RONALD REAGAN

UP_close:_

RONALD REAGAN

a twentieth-century life by
JAMES SUTHERLAND

VIKING

VIKING

Published by Penguin Group

Penguin Young Readers Group, 345 Hudson Street, New York, New York 10014, U.S.A.

Penguin Group (Canada), 90 Eglinton Avenue East, Suite 700, Toronto, Ontario,
Canada M4P 2Y3 (a division of Pearson Penguin Canada Inc.)

Penguin Books Ltd, 80 Strand, London WC2R 0RL, England

Penguin Ireland, 25 St Stephen's Green, Dublin 2, Ireland (a division of Penguin Books Ltd)

Penguin Group (Australia), 250 Camberwell Road, Camberwell, Victoria 3124, Australia
(a division of Pearson Australia Group Pty Ltd)

Penguin Books India Pvt Ltd, 11 Community Centre, Panchsheel Park, New Delhi – 110 017, India

Penguin Group (NZ), 67 Apollo Drive, Rosedale, North Shore 0632, New Zealand
(a division of Pearson New Zealand Ltd)

Penguin Books (South Africa) (Pty) Ltd, 24 Sturdee Avenue, Rosebank, Johannesburg 2196,
South Africa

Penguin Books Ltd, Registered Offices: 80 Strand, London WC2R 0RL, England

First published in 2008 by Viking, a division of Penguin Young Readers Group

10 9 8 7 6 5 4 3 2 1

Photo credits can be found on page 253

LIBRARY OF CONGRESS CATALOGING-IN-PUBLICATION DATA
Sutherland, James, date–
Up close : Ronald Reagan / James Sutherland.
p. cm. — (Up close)
ISBN 978-0-670-06345-1 (hardcover)
1. Reagan, Ronald—Juvenile literature. 2. Presidents—United States—Biography—
Juvenile literature. I. Title.
E877.S885 2008
973.927092—dc22
[B]
2008021328

Printed in the U.S.A.
Set in Goudy
Book design by Jim Hoover

Oriole Park Branch
7454 W. Balmoral Ave.
Chicago, IL 60656
312-744-1965
Mon-Thur 9-9
Fri & Sat 9-5; Sun Closed

To my wife. If I had known when we met that you were going to make each day seem like a wonderful adventure where everything is possible, I would have asked you out even sooner. Thank you for everything.

CONTENTS

FOREWORD

I'M PRETTY SURE my parents thought there was something wrong with me when I was ten years old. I was not a normal kid.

Normal boys had posters of sports stars on the walls of their bedrooms. I had pictures of America's fortieth president. Ronald Reagan was my hero.

When Reagan ran for reelection in 1984, I had my first taste of politics. I loved it. I subscribed to *Time* magazine so I could read about the campaign each week. (My parents didn't realize what I had done until the bill arrived.) I didn't have much of a grasp of the issues in the campaign, but I knew that Reagan made me feel proud to be an American. When he spoke about this country, he made it sound like a special place, an example to the world of what freedom meant. He was such an incredible communicator, who inspired you and made you feel like he was a friend. I called him Ronnie.

As I grew older, I kept following Ronnie's every move. I started to gain an understanding of his beliefs and politics, his desire for a smaller government and a strong foreign policy. When I was fourteen, I was chosen to play the part of George H. W. Bush, Ronnie's vice president, who was running to succeed him, in a mock debate at school. For an hour, I spoke about what "I" would do in office. I wore a tiny Ronnie doll clipped to my tie for good luck.

A year later, I traveled to the Soviet Union on a summer exchange program. If Ronnie was able to make peace with Soviet leader Mikhail Gorbachev, maybe the Soviets weren't the strange, villainous people all of us growing up during the Cold War were taught to believe. A summer with Russian kids taught me that the world was a big place, but most people were friendly if you attempted to reach out to them and understand their point of view.

Later, my political views changed. I became pretty liberal for a while, then more moderate. Then I became a political reporter. People ask me if most political reporters are Republicans or Democrats, but I think most of us belong to the Skeptical Party. We're skeptical of all politicians.

But Reagan continued to fascinate me. He was an enigma. People close to him never really knew what he was thinking. On the surface he seemed like a simple man, but the truth is he was complicated. He had a difficult childhood but pursued his dreams until he was a movie star and then president. He was underestimated for most of his political career but found a way to succeed. What was his secret? Who was the real Reagan?

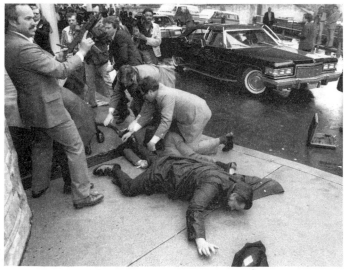

INTRODUCTION

MONDAY, MARCH 30, 1981.

The president of the United States had been shot and was close to death, and all he could think to do was crack jokes.

At 2:25 P.M., Ronald Reagan had finished giving a speech at a union meeting at the Washington Hilton Hotel. The Republican president, in office for just two months, left the hotel by a side entrance, escorted by Secret Service. Just before he got to his car, a noise that sounded like firecrackers rang out. "What the hell's that?" Reagan asked.

Suddenly, a Secret Service agent grabbed Reagan

Top: Reagan leaving the Washington Hilton Hotel seconds before an assassination attempt.
Bottom: The scene immediately after the assassination attempt. James Brady and police officer Thomas Delahanty lie wounded on the ground.

by the waist and threw him into the back of the limo, then jumped on top of him. Reagan felt a horrible pain in his back. "Jerry, get off, I think you've broken one of my ribs," he gasped. Jerry Parr, the lead agent assigned to protect Reagan, yelled to the driver to take them to the White House. He got off Reagan, who sat up, coughed into his hand, and saw blood. "You not only broke a rib, I think the rib punctured my lung," Reagan said. Parr yelled to the driver to take them to George Washington University Hospital, the nearest in the area.

Reagan was coughing up blood, soaking his handkerchief red. No matter how hard he tried to breathe, he couldn't get enough air. But as the car pulled up to the emergency room entrance, the president insisted on walking in. With great effort, he got out of the car, buttoned his jacket, and walked twenty feet. As soon as he got inside, he collapsed. Doctors and nurses crowded around him, loading him on a gurney, wheeling him to an empty room, and cutting off all his clothes. "I can't breathe," Reagan said, and then he passed out.

Reagan continued to slip in and out of consciousness as the doctors tried to determine the extent of his injuries. A nurse noticed a small slit under the president's left armpit. It was a bullet hole.

Reagan's wife, Nancy, had arrived at the hospital ten minutes after he got there, but could not enter his room until his breathing stabilized. When she did, he opened his eyes, saw her, and said, "Honey, I forgot to duck."

At 3:24 P.M., doctors wheeled Reagan into the operating room. The bullet was still inside him. As he was rolled by James Baker, his chief of staff, he winked at him. He passed his friend Senator Paul Laxalt and said, "Don't worry about me. I'll make it."

Reagan was unconscious as the doctor widened the incision under his arm and inched a catheter in. After searching carefully, the doctor found the bullet. It had hit the limo, flattened like a dime, ricocheted off, and entered the president's body. It hit one of his ribs and stopped less than an inch from his heart. One inch farther and he would have been dead.

He could have died regardless—even after they removed the bullet, the doctors could not stop the bleeding. Reagan had already lost ten pints of blood.

He was alive only because they were transfusing blood into him, and because Reagan was in great physical shape for a seventy-year-old man. They would need to operate again shortly, opening up his chest this time. While they were preparing, and before they administered more anesthetic, Reagan opened his eyes. "I hope you're a Republican," he said to the doctor closest to him. The doctor responded, "Mr. President, we're all Republicans today."

At 6:20 P.M., the doctors finished operating. They had stopped the bleeding but weren't sure if the president would live. An hour later Reagan woke up in severe pain and was given medication. He would stay in the hospital for thirteen days before he was stable enough to go back to the White House.

The American people found out only later how close they had come to losing their president. And they learned that Reagan faced death the same way he approached life—with courage, determination, and an incurable sense of optimism.

ONE

AT ELEVEN YEARS old, Ronald Reagan walked up to his house one evening to find his father passed out on the porch.

"I came home from the YMCA one cold blustery winter's night," Ronald later wrote. "My mother was gone on one of her sewing jobs and I expected the house to be empty. As I walked up the stairs, I nearly stumbled over a lump near the front door; it was Jack lying in the snow, his arms outstretched, flat on his back. I leaned over to see what was wrong and smelled whiskey."

Ronald's father, Jack, was an alcoholic. It was an addiction that Jack struggled with for most of his life, and it led him to fight with his wife, have trouble at work, and sometimes leave home for short periods.

Ronald's mother, Nelle, had explained to him and his older brother, Neil, why their father disappeared sometimes. "She said Jack had a sickness that he couldn't control—an addiction to alcohol. She said he fought it but sometimes lost control and we shouldn't love him any less because of it because it was something he couldn't control."

That night on the porch, with his mother and Neil not there, Ronald had to deal with his father's sickness on his own. "For a moment or two, I looked down at him and thought about continuing on into the house and going to bed, as if he weren't there. But I couldn't do it." The eleven-year-old boy grabbed his father's coat, pulled him into the house, and put him in bed.

Ronald Reagan always described his childhood as the happy story of a boy in small-town America—a wholesome coming-of-age in the Midwest. "As I look back on those days in Dixon[, Illinois,] I think my life was as sweet and idyllic as it could be," he wrote in his 1990 autobiography. But Ronald's early years were more complicated than idyllic. His father's alcoholism sometimes spurred his mother to take Ronald and Neil away to stay with her relatives.

The Reagan family Christmas card photo, 1916. From left: Jack, Neil, Ronald, and Nelle.

Those years had two effects on young Ronald. Early on he decided that he would never dwell on the negative. His mother, a deeply religious woman, had taught him that God made everything happen for a reason. The second effect was more subtle. Psychologists have suggested that children of alcoholics have trouble developing close relationships with people. Because their parents act unpredictably, often fight, and hurt their children's feelings, children of alcoholics try to avoid getting hurt by not allowing themselves to get too close emotionally to anyone. Ronald had a huge heart and cared about almost all people deeply, but he was a loner.

Ronald Wilson Reagan was born February 6, 1911, in a second-story apartment in the little town of Tampico, Illinois, about 120 miles west of Chicago. Ronald's nickname growing up was Dutch. According to family legend, the night he was born, his father said, "He looks like a fat little Dutchman." It's more likely he got the nickname as a toddler because he had a moplike haircut that people called a "Dutch boy." Another story was that he gave it to himself as a boy simply because he didn't like being called Ronald.

When Dutch was born, the delivery had been difficult, and the doctor warned Nelle that she shouldn't have any more children. It would be just the four of them, which Dutch later said made them all very close. He and his brother, two years older, even called their parents by their first names once they became teenagers.

Dutch's father, John Edward Reagan, known as Jack, was orphaned at age six and spent his childhood constantly on the move, living with various relatives in several towns on the Mississippi River, working instead of going to school. He had little formal education, and he and his three siblings rarely saw one another. Jack compensated for always being the new guy by telling stories and jokes, trying to win people over. "No one I ever met could tell a story better," Dutch later wrote. "My dad was destined by God, I think, to become a salesman."

Jack worked for most of his life as a clerk in general stores, but his real dream was to be a shoe salesman and have his own store. As an adult he never settled down, restlessly moving his family from town to town, and store to store.

Even though Dutch would later write about his

frustration with his father's drinking, he loved Jack and admired him for certain qualities. His father was a strong believer in treating people equally. Jack was of Irish descent and a Catholic, and in those days some Americans discriminated against Irish Catholics. Jack taught his boys to treat all people the same. He once told them of a night when he was traveling for work. After he checked into a hotel, he was told that though he was welcome, the hotel did not allow Jews. Jack walked out and slept in his car.

Dutch also said that his father was a cynic who tended to expect the worst from people. Nelle was the exact opposite. "She always expected to find the best in people and often did, even among the prisoners at our local jail to whom she frequently brought hot meals." But despite their differences, Reagan's parents loved each other very much.

Nelle Wilson had also been born in northwestern Illinois and, like Jack, left school early. At one point she worked in a store owned by one of Jack's aunts, where she most likely met her future husband. They were married in 1904. Nelle was always a performer—acting, reading, writing—and when she was younger she was quite a dancer.

A few years after she was married, but before Dutch was born, Nelle found a new faith, joining a Protestant church denomination called the Christian Church, also known as the Disciples of Christ. According to her granddaughter Maureen, the conversion was sparked when Nelle had a near-death experience and decided afterward to devote her life to Jesus.

The Disciples did not believe in dancing, but they did believe in learning, reading, and acting. They also opposed drinking of any kind, which might have been one of the attractions to Nelle after seeing what alcohol was doing to her husband. More importantly, every town the Reagans moved to had a chapter of the Disciples, which gave Nelle a stable home on Sundays.

Dutch once said that while he may not have grown up on the wrong side of the tracks, it was close enough to hear the train. The Reagan family struggled to make ends meet. Neil later remembered that when he was young, he and Dutch would go down to the store with a dime on Saturday morning and ask the butcher for some liver "for the cat." But they didn't own a cat. Liver was cheap because most people wouldn't eat it. The boys would bring it home, and Nelle would cook it for Sunday night dinner.

Moving so much didn't make life any easier. When Dutch was three, the family moved to the big city—Chicago—but a year later they moved again, this time to Galesburg. When Dutch was seven, they moved to Monmouth; when he was eight, back to Tampico; and when he was nine, they moved to Dixon, where Dutch would spend the rest of his childhood. But even in Dixon, Jack wasn't totally settled—the family moved to five different homes there.

It would have been easy for a boy growing up like Dutch did to end up like his dad—restless and troubled. "I was a little introverted and probably a little slow in making really close friends. In some ways I think this reluctance to get close to people has never left me completely. I've never had trouble making friends, but I've been inclined to hold back a little of myself, reserving it for myself."

Dixon, Illinois, sits on the Rock River, about one hundred miles west of Chicago. When the Reagans arrived in 1920, it was home to about eight thousand people. It had a few factories, including a cement plant, but dairy farms dominated the landscape. Jack moved his family there because a wealthy business acquaintance who liked Jack had partnered with him to open a shoe store. Jack's partner put up the money to buy the store, and Jack put up his time as the store's full-time manager. They split the profits. It was a dream come true for Jack.

Life in Dixon was much like life elsewhere at first, for Dutch. He spent much of his time alone. He liked to wander the woods near the river, pretending he was a cowboy or a fur trapper. He became a doodler, sketching little cartoons to amuse himself. He also got a library card and began taking out big piles of books, mostly adventure stories about Tarzan and other heroes. Reading and memorizing came easily to Dutch, and he did well in school. He even skipped second grade completely.

Dutch's favorite book was *That Printer of Udell's*, by Harold Bell Wright. This was a novel that told the story of a young man in the Midwest who ends up running away from home after his alcoholic father kills his mother. The boy finds God and begins doing good works, helping reform his adopted town. Eventually he is elected to Congress and leaves to reform Washington, D.C.

The book had a powerful impact on Dutch, as he explained in a letter to the author's daughter-in-law he wrote more than sixty years later. "I found a role model in that traveling printer. He set me on a course I've tried to follow even unto this day. After reading it and thinking about it for a few days, I went to my mother and told her I wanted to be baptized." Dutch was baptized just days later as a Disciple of Christ, and he belonged to the Christian Church for the rest of his life.

At church meetings and during charity projects, Nelle liked to use her talents as a performer. And she convinced young Dutch to memorize a short speech and recite it in front of an audience. "I don't remember what I said," Reagan would later write, "but I'll never forget the response: People laughed and applauded. For a kid suffering childhood pangs of insecurity, the applause was music."

One Sunday when Dutch was thirteen, Jack took the family for a drive. Dutch saw his mother's glasses lying near him in the backseat, and he playfully put them on. "The next instant, I let out a yelp that almost caused Jack to run off the road. I'd discovered a world I didn't know existed before." No one had realized it, but Dutch was extremely nearsighted—anything farther than a few feet in front of his face was blurry. The next day he saw a doctor who fitted him with a big pair of glasses. They were ugly, with black frames, but he could see.

Now Dutch was determined to succeed in sports. But at a year younger than most students starting high school, Dutch was only five feet three inches tall and 108 pounds. He was the smallest boy trying out for the football team. He didn't make the cut. But the next year, he did. By his junior year, the young offensive lineman was just over six feet tall.

While Dutch loved football, his best sport was swimming, and the summer after his junior year, he got a job as a lifeguard at Lowell Park, a beautiful, wooded spot on the Rock River, three miles north of town. The river was very swift—treacherous in places. During the next six summers Dutch saved seventy-seven people from drowning. But it was not a glamorous job. He had to wake up early seven days a week. At the park, he would watch the beach, the river, and the swimmers—on busy days as many as one thousand people. The park didn't close until ten P.M. He was paid fifteen dollars a week the first summer.

Back in school, Dutch's English teacher liked some of Dutch's essays so much that he began asking him to read them aloud. His classmates laughed at and applauded his creative stories and his entertaining way of delivering them. When the teacher began directing school plays, he urged Dutch to audition. An added motivation for Dutch was that Margaret Cleaver, a girl he had a crush on, was cast to play the lead female part. He had known Margaret for a few years—her father was a minister at Dutch's church. Dutch got the lead role, and soon, Margaret was his girlfriend.

By Dutch's senior year, he was no longer the shy kid who spent his time alone. He was elected student body president, starred in all the school plays, and played both offense and defense for the football team. In his senior yearbook, he put a line from a poem he had written next to his photo: "Life is just one grand sweet song, so start the music."

TWO

JACK HAD ALWAYS encouraged his sons to get a college education, but he warned them that he did not have enough money to pay for it. Two years earlier, Neil had graduated from Dixon High and gone to work at the cement plant. Dutch had not applied anywhere, but with four hundred dollars in savings from his lifeguard work, he hopped into Margaret's car on a September day in 1928, and the two drove ninety-five miles south to Eureka, Illinois, home of Eureka College. Founded in the early 1800s by the Disciples of Christ, Eureka was a tiny school, with fewer than two hundred students. Margaret had already been accepted.

The day after they arrived on campus, while Margaret signed up for classes, Dutch went to see the dean of students to talk his way into college. After hearing about Reagan's financial situation, Dean Samuel Harrod took the young man to see the football coach, who agreed to give Reagan a ninety-dollar-a-year scholarship in return for him competing at both football and swimming. Harrod then convinced the members of the Tau Kappa Epsilon fraternity to take Reagan as a pledge and give him a job washing dishes. That earned him free meals at the house. Between those savings and Reagan's lifeguard money, he was able to enroll as Eureka's newest student. Dutch had to scrimp and save at every opportunity, but he managed it. During his sophomore year, he was even able to help Neil enroll.

Dutch chose economics as his major, but he admitted he majored unofficially in extracurricular activities. "Although my grades were higher than average," Dutch later wrote, "my principal academic ambition at Eureka was to maintain the C average I needed to remain eligible for football, swimming, track, and the other school activities I participated in—two years in the student senate, three years as basketball cheerleader, three years as president of the Eureka Boosters Club, two years as yearbook features editor, and, during my last year, student body president and captain and coach of the swim team."

Though Dutch recounted many stories about his activities at school in his autobiographies, he wrote almost nothing about his time in class. Years later, he visited Eureka and accepted an honorary degree, joking that he had always felt the first degree was honorary.

In sports, Dutch quickly established himself as the best swimmer on campus. His first year on the football team was mostly spent on the bench, but after that he started. Off the field, Dutch impressed his teammates with his enthusiasm and his good nature. One player remarked years later that Dutch "had a personality that would sweep you off your feet." After tough games or practices, he would entertain them in the locker room or on the bus back to school by picking up a broom and pretending it was a microphone and he was a sportscaster.

In 1931, the Eureka team traveled to another town in Illinois for a game. The bus stopped at a hotel, and Coach Ralph McKinzie went inside to get rooms for everyone. He was gone for so long that Dutch went to find him. McKinzie was at the hotel front desk, arguing with the manager, who was telling the coach that all the white football players could stay there, but the team's two black players—William Franklin Burghardt and Jim Rattan—were not welcome. Furious at this racism, the coach decided the entire team would sleep on the bus.

But Dutch told the coach that Burghardt and Rattan might be embarrassed that their teammates would have to do that. He mentioned that his hometown was not far away and suggested that he and the two players take a cab to his house in Dixon. They were welcome in his parents' home. Burghardt would never forget the warm welcome he received from Nelle and Jack—he stayed friends with Dutch for the rest of his life.

Dutch was not a football star, but he was a natural at one of his other passions: acting. During a vacation in his freshman year, Dutch joined Margaret and her parents to go see a touring play from London. He was so moved by the performance that he decided he wanted to become a professional actor. From then on he auditioned for every play at Eureka.

By the time Dutch graduated in 1932, he and Margaret were engaged, and he planned to be an actor. But things weren't that simple. Margaret had an offer to teach high school in another town. Dutch had no job offers. The couple would keep in touch by mail, for the time being. Dutch went home to work as a lifeguard, with no idea what he would do when summer ended.

Dutch wasn't the only American worried about his future. In 1932, the nation was three years into what became known as the Great Depression. The 1920s had been a time of economic prosperity—as big cities grew, factories went up, and people spent plenty of money on homes and cars or investing in stocks. Many people borrowed money for big purchases. But in October 1929, the stock market crashed, and stocks lost a large percentage of their value in a matter of hours. Over the next month, the market continued to decline.

The market crash may not have been the only cause of the Depression, but it was a major factor. It wiped out many people's savings, and many banks went out of business. Soon more than 25 percent of American workers were unemployed—thirteen million people. By 1930, economic trouble had spread around the world. It was truly a worldwide Depression.

The U.S. government hadn't proven to people that

it could help. President Hoover believed that the best policy for government was to leave business alone. His administration had kept regulations and taxes on corporations low—this had helped during the boom times. But as the country slid deeper into a depression, many Americans felt that their government had abandoned them. As Dutch would remember later, "Those were cheerless desperate days. I don't think anyone who did not live through the Depression can ever understand how difficult it was."

Dixon was as hard hit as any town, and Jack's shoe store had not been spared. In 1929, while both of his sons were still at Eureka, he had to close the store for good. He and Nelle moved out of their house and into a two-room apartment. They sublet the second room. Jack took a job in Springfield, Illinois, 150 miles away, managing a small store. Nelle stayed in Dixon, working in a seamstress's shop and sewing clothes for neighbors to earn extra cash. At one point, she called Dutch and asked him for fifty dollars. They were out of money and the grocery bill was due. Dutch sent the money, part of his savings from a previous summer.

While he spent his summer after graduation as a

lifeguard, Dutch tried to figure out what to do for a job. He didn't see a way to become an actor, but maybe as a stepping-stone he could get a job in radio. In the 1930s, there was no such thing as television, so most Americans listened to the radio or went to the movies for entertainment and news. But Dutch didn't know how to get a radio job. A businessman vacationing at Lowell Park suggested that Dutch visit radio stations and offer to take any job, just to get his foot in the door.

At the end of the summer, Dutch hitchhiked to Chicago and visited every station in town. No one was interested in hiring him. Plenty of people with radio experience were looking for jobs—why would a station hire a newcomer? At one station, a secretary told Dutch that he was wasting his time in Chicago. He would be better off going to a smaller city where a station might give an untested rookie a chance.

Dutch returned home to Dixon dejected, but he was not going to give up. He decided to take the secretary's advice, so he asked Jack if he could borrow his car. Jack encouraged his son, and Dutch drove off one day in October.

Dutch traveled seventy-five miles west to the tricities area, a cluster of three towns straddling the Mississippi River in Illinois and Iowa. After striking out with stations on the Illinois side, he crossed the river to Davenport, Iowa, home to a small station called WOC. Dutch met with Pete MacArthur, program manager. MacArthur asked the young man where he'd been. He'd been looking for an announcer for a month and filled the job the day before. Hurt and frustrated, Dutch walked out, saying, "How in the hell does a guy ever get to be a sports announcer if he can't get inside a station?"

At that, MacArthur stopped him. The little Scottish man with a thick accent looked up at Dutch and asked him if he knew anything about football. Dutch told him that he'd played for seven years in high school and college. "Could ye tell me about a football game and make me see it as if I was home listening on the radio?" Dutch bravely said yes. So MacArthur led him to a studio, stood him in front of a microphone, and told him that when the little red light went on, he should start describing a game. MacArthur then went into a control room next door.

Dutch stood at the mike and tried to think of the most exciting game he had been a part of. There was the game in his last season at Eureka when his team had won in the last twenty seconds thanks to a sixty-five-yard touchdown run by the quarterback. The light went on, and Dutch started talking. "Here we are in the fourth quarter with Western State University leading Eureka College six to nothing. Long blue shadows are settling over the field. . . ." When he ended the broadcast, MacArthur came into the room and told him he was great. He wanted him to return on Saturday to announce the Iowa–Minnesota homecoming football game. He would pay Dutch five dollars.

Happy and excited, Dutch returned home and read everything he could over the next few days about Iowa's and Minnesota's players. On Saturday, he took the bus to Davenport, and he and MacArthur drove to the game in Iowa City. At the end of the game MacArthur told him he could come back to announce the remaining three Iowa games for ten dollars a game. But after those three games, MacArthur had no more work for Dutch.

Things were not getting easier at home. On

Christmas Eve, a special-delivery letter arrived for Jack—it was word he was fired.

In February, MacArthur called—one of WOC's announcers had quit, and MacArthur wanted Dutch to take over. He was going to be a radio announcer. Dutch told him he would be in Davenport the next day, and eagerly wrote a letter to Margaret to tell her the news.

One month after Dutch moved to Davenport, another man began a new job. On March 4, 1933, Franklin Delano Roosevelt took the oath of office and became America's thirty-second president. A Democrat, Roosevelt had run against Herbert Hoover by promising "a new deal" for Americans that would ease their economic suffering. During Roosevelt's first one hundred days, he sent a lengthy list of bills to Congress, all of which passed easily. The bills created numerous new agencies that offered economic aid and created jobs. Roosevelt and his administration tried a lot of ideas, in hope of finding something that would help.

At his inauguration, Roosevelt said, "The only thing we have to fear is fear itself." He knew that a major factor behind the Depression was Americans' lack of confidence in the economy and their own futures. One reason for his flurry of activity during his first one hundred days in office was to make the country feel it was moving forward. He began giving a series of "fireside chats"—evening radio addresses to the people, during which he would outline his ideas and try to promote confidence.

Jack was a Democrat and had brought his sons up to be Democrats. At age twenty-one in 1932, Dutch had cast his first vote for president, for Roosevelt. And as a young announcer starting out in radio, he admired a president who knew the power of the medium to reach out to people. "During his fireside chats, his strong, gentle, confident voice resonated across the nation with an eloquence that brought comfort and resilience and reassured us that we could lick any problem," he later wrote. When Roosevelt visited Iowa a few years later, Dutch eagerly waited by a window for a glimpse of the president's car as it went by.

By the time Roosevelt gave his first fireside chat in March 1933, Dutch was a month into his new job on WOC. He struggled at first. While he had been good at ad-libbing during football games, announcing meant reading a lot of material on the air, and Dutch initially had a hard time sounding like he was having a conversation with listeners. He just sounded like he was reading aloud.

But with practice, Dutch began to develop a more conversational radio style, and once he did, people grew to love his voice. Dutch made listeners feel like they were his friends. He was also earning one hundred dollars a month, some of which he sent to his parents and some of which he sent to Neil at Eureka. In May, WOC's owner decided to merge the station with sister station WHO in Des Moines. Dutch and MacArthur moved west to Iowa's capital.

Back in Dixon, Jack finally got a job. When Roosevelt became president and began creating agencies to help end the Depression, members of his administration went looking for Democrats in each town to help implement the agencies' plans. Most people in Dixon were Republicans. Jack was one of the few Democrats in town, so he was hired as a supervisor at the Civil Works Administration to help find jobs for the unemployed in Dixon.

Dutch on the air at radio station WHO in Des Moines, Iowa, circa 1935.

When Dutch moved to Des Moines, he called Margaret to tell her. They had visited each other occasionally, but their relationship was growing distant. Late in 1933, Margaret and one of her sisters took a trip to Europe. Soon after, she sent Dutch a letter with his engagement ring inside. She had met a man in Europe who worked for the U.S. State Department and they were getting married. "Margaret's decision shattered me," Dutch later wrote, "not so much I think, because she no longer loved me, but because I no longer had anyone to love."

Dutch started dating again soon, but never the same woman for very long. His heart was broken. But he did make several new friends in Des Moines, most of them students at Drake College, another Disciples school. They hung out at a bar named Cy's Moonlight Inn—he liked meeting girls there, but drank very little. (Many Disciples drank, despite the church's tenet—Dutch drank throughout his life, though never heavily.) He also swam almost every day, and a friend at the radio station, Myrtle Williams, taught him how to ride horses. He quickly fell in love with horses, and riding became a way for him to spend time alone and clear his thoughts.

Dutch continued to stay close to his family, and in 1934, Neil visited him. WHO's owner was reopening the WOC station in Davenport and needed new staff. Dutch arranged an audition for Neil for an announcer's slot, and he got the job, moved to Davenport, and eventually became a manager at the station. Nelle frequently came to Des Moines to see her son. But in 1936, she called with bad news—Jack had suffered a heart attack. His heart was weak after decades of smoking and drinking. He was okay, but he needed rest and could not work. Dutch regularly sent money home to support them both.

Over time Dutch became incredibly popular for his radio broadcasts. He announced many programs but was best known for his sports coverage, especially baseball games. WHO broadcast Chicago Cubs and Chicago White Sox games—150 games a year, all featuring Dutch. But he never went to Chicago for the games. Instead, he sat in a studio, next to a man named Curly, who wore headphones. Someone at the game in Chicago would send telegraph signals of what happened in the game to Curly, who would type a code on a slip of paper and hand it to Dutch. "It might contain the information S2C," Dutch later wrote. "Without a pause I would translate this into 'It's a called strike breaking over the inside corner, making it two strikes on the batter.'" Because the audience could not see the game, Dutch had to paint a picture for them with words, describing every bit of action at the stadium—action he couldn't see. "If the Cubs were in the field, I would continue while I waited for the next [slip of paper], saying, 'Hartnett returns the ball to Lon Warneke, Warneke is dusting his hands in the resin, steps back up on the mound, is getting the sign again from Hartnett, here's the pitch.'"

Over six hundred times a game, Dutch went through this process. The fans knew he wasn't in Chicago, but they didn't care. They loved listening to Dutch's version of the game. Even if the details were not completely accurate, the results and the drama of Dutch's account were what mattered. Dutch knew how to grab their attention and hold it with his words.

One day, however, Dutch's talent had a big test. "I saw Curly start to type so I finished the windup and had [the pitcher] send the ball on its way to the plate, took the slip from Curly, and found myself faced with the terse note: 'The wire has gone dead.'"

Not wanting to break the spell, and not wanting to lose his listeners to another station during a ball game that was tied in the ninth inning, Dutch quickly thought of one thing that could happen that wouldn't show up in the box score the next day. He said the batter had fouled off the ball. He looked at Curly, who shrugged helplessly, and then he said the batter fouled off the next pitch, describing at length some kids fighting for the ball. For more than five minutes, he described the batter repeatedly fouling off pitches, growing more and more nervous that he might have the batter set a record for foul balls. Finally, when it was unbearable, Curly started typing again—the wire had come back to life. He handed Dutch a slip. It said the batter had popped out on the first pitch.

Thanks to his radio broadcasts, Dutch was a celebrity in large parts of the Midwest. He had a regular sports column in a Des Moines newspaper. Civic groups asked him to give speeches at their events. The sponsors of his baseball games asked him to speak at meetings of businessmen in Chicago and other cities. Dutch filled most of these speeches with funny stories of mishaps on the radio. He could have happily stayed at WHO, but he had bigger dreams. He still wanted to act and decided to test the waters in Hollywood.

Every year in February and March, the Chicago Cubs went to Catalina, an island just off the coast of Los Angeles, for spring training. Dutch convinced WHO to send him along with the team for ten days in 1937. He told WHO he was going because he wanted to cover the Cubs. But he may have been planning a chance to jump into the movies all along. While in L.A. one night, he met Joy Hodges for dinner. Hodges had been a singer at WHO, but she had moved to Hollywood and gotten some small parts in films. As they ate dinner together that night, Dutch confessed that he had always wanted to be in movies.

"Take off your glasses," she said. Hodges explained that movie studios weren't interested in actors who wore glasses, so she wanted to see what he looked like without them. Dutch took them off, and Hodges looked at his face. She smiled and told him she knew an agent who would tell Dutch if he had a chance as an actor. The next morning, Dutch was sitting in the office of agent George Ward, with his glasses in his pocket, explaining why he thought he could be in movies. Ward listened, picked up the phone, and called the casting director at Warner Brothers Studios, Max Arnow.

The next thing Dutch knew, he was sitting in front of Arnow, being examined by the casting director. Arnow thought Dutch looked like a nice clean-cut, all-American man. But most of all, he liked Dutch's voice. So Dutch took a screen test. He was given a script from a scene, quickly memorized the lines, and then acted it out on camera with a young actress. Arnow thought he performed perfectly, but studio head Jack Warner had to see the film before Dutch could be hired. Ward, now his agent, told Dutch to stay in L.A. for a few days. But Dutch explained that spring training was ending—he needed to get back to Des Moines.

He took the train home, staring out the window, wondering if he had just made the biggest mistake of his life. But two days later, on March 22, 1937, a telegram arrived in Des Moines from Ward. Warner Bros. had offered Dutch a seven-year contract for two hundred dollars a week. Ward wanted to know what he should do. It was a standard contract, and exactly what Dutch had dreamed of—he was going to be an actor. He immediately wired back, "Sign before they change their minds . . . Dutch Reagan."

THREE

DUTCH'S FRIENDS AT WHO threw him a party the night before he left for Hollywood. It was broadcast over the radio, and the mayor came to say good-bye to the city's favorite announcer. The next day, Dutch climbed into his convertible and drove west toward California.

On his first day at the studio, Arnow and other staffers gave Dutch a thorough transformation, turning the radio host into a film actor. First he was sent to hair and makeup, where his hairstyle was changed. Next up was wardrobe, where they told Dutch his neck looked too short for his head and shoulders and ordered specially tailored shirts for him. As for his glasses, Dutch would just take them off while filming scenes. Eventually, he tried out a new technology called contact lenses.

Finally, Arnow and the studio publicists decided his name had to go. Dutch Reagan was not going to work on a movie poster. They looked him over and tried to pick a fake name that Dutch "looked like." Finally, Dutch himself spoke up. "How about Ronald?" He figured he would rather have his real name if he couldn't have Dutch. After repeating Ronald Reagan a few times, the publicists approved. At twenty-six years old, Ronald Reagan was once again Ronald Reagan.

Before filming his first scene, Ronald learned that a seven-year contract didn't necessarily guarantee seven years of work. Warner Bros. had an option to terminate the contract after six months or a year if Ronald's acting didn't work out. Ronald felt a lot of pressure, especially since he hadn't really acted since college. His first film was called *Love Is on the Air*. In the movie, Ronald played a part he knew well—a radio announcer in a small town. Several of Reagan's early roles were similar to his personality—clean-cut, all-American. Hollywood often typecast actors until they proved they could handle more challenging parts. Ronald quickly proved ideal for films. He was a natural on-screen, but what the studio liked most was his ability to memorize lines quickly and work fast without putting up much of a fuss.

While filming his first few movies, Ronald paid particular attention to how movies were made—the director's work, the cameras and lights. He also learned what made for a good scene. He was willing to tell a director to cut one of his lines if he thought it would make a scene flow better. That was a rarity in Hollywood, where the number of lines showed how big a star you were.

By the end of 1937, Ronald was settled in Hollywood. Warner Bros. wasn't going to terminate his contract—in fact, the studio gave him a raise. He called Jack and Nelle and asked them to move out and join him, buying them a house near his apartment. He missed them, and they had little reason to stay in Dixon. Jack could no longer hold most jobs because of his heart condition, so Ronald gave him a new one—answering his fan mail. Nelle quickly joined the Beverly Hills branch of the Christian Church, which Ronald attended every Sunday, and started volunteering for local charities. Ronald had dinner with them several nights a week.

With Ronald's encouragement, Neil and his wife, Bess, soon followed, and Neil got a job at a Los Angeles radio station, first as an announcer, and then as a director. One night, three of Ronald's old friends in Des Moines were talking of what Ronald had told them about life in Los Angeles and decided to move west, too. A huge number of people from Illinois and Iowa were moving to Southern California—even the current governor of the state had grown up in Iowa. Ronald was able to re-create much of the life he had had in the Midwest, but in different surroundings. He and his friends would go to the beach now and swim in the Pacific Ocean or play golf—though Reagan never became a huge fan of the sport. At night, they went to the movies.

In 1938, Ronald made a movie called *Brother Rat* and became friends with one of his costars, a twenty-year-old actress named Jane Wyman. One day, Jane and Ronald were supposed to have photos taken for a publicity campaign for the movie, but the photographer was nowhere to be found. As they waited, they chatted about where they were from. Jane grew increasingly impatient about the photographer's tardiness, but she marveled at how calm Ronald was. Nothing seemed to bother him or change his cheerful demeanor. She had never met someone so self-assured.

Jane was quickly infatuated with Ronald, but he was not interested in dating. It had been five years since Margaret Cleaver had mailed his ring back to him, and Ronald had not had another serious relationship. Jane decided that if wooing him didn't work, she would woo those around him. She started hanging out with his friends from Des Moines, going to the beach or to the movies with all of them. She became friends with Nelle, too, and even began attending church with her.

Jane had been born in 1917 in Missouri and was originally named Sarah Jane Mayfield. Her childhood was not easy—when she was five, her father died and her mother left Sarah Jane with a couple who lived next door and moved away. Sarah Jane began performing on the radio at age thirteen, and by fifteen she was working in Hollywood in films as a chorus girl, claiming she was three years older. She changed her last name to Wyman. When she met Ronald, Jane was also being typecast by Warner Bros., usually as a goofy cute blonde. She wanted roles that were more dramatic.

In 1939, Hollywood gossip columnist Louella Parsons invited Ronald, Jane, and other promising actors on a stage tour of America for nine weeks. Together on the road, Ronald and Jane grew even closer and began dating seriously. One day, Jane went to Parsons and told her a big scoop—she and Ronald were engaged. They were married in January 1940, and held the reception at Parsons's house. They moved into Jane's apartment, and studio publicists were soon sending press releases to magazines about the wholesome young couple.

Also in 1940, Ronald made the movie that got him out of lesser pictures and into big roles. As a sports fan from the Midwest, Ronald had long been fascinated by the story of Knute Rockne, the late football coach of the University of Notre Dame. He learned that Warner Bros. was developing a film about the coach, titled *Knute Rockne—All American*. Pat O'Brien was cast to play Rockne, but Ronald was interested in the part of George Gipp, who had been one of Rockne's most talented players before dying of pneumonia in 1920. Eight years after his death, when Notre Dame's football team was having a rough season, Rockne inspired his players for a game against West Point by telling them how Gipp had told Rockne on his deathbed, "Some time, Rock, when the team is up against it, when things are wrong and the breaks are beating the boys, ask them to go in there with all they've got and win just one for the Gipper. I don't know where I'll be then, Rock. But I'll know about it, and I'll be happy." Notre Dame won the game.

Ronald was not being considered for the role, but he thought he was perfect for it and asked O'Brien for help. O'Brien convinced Jack Warner to give Ronald an audition based on Ronald's experience playing football. O'Brien and Ronald filmed a screen test together and after Warner saw it, he gave Ronald the part. The film was a big success, and though O'Brien got much of the attention, Ronald won newfound fame for his portrayal of Gipp and his deathbed speech to Rockne. From then on, people sometimes called Ronald "the Gipper," and he enjoyed telling them to "win one for the Gipper."

The movie premiere was held at Notre Dame, and Ronald decided to bring Jack with him. Notre Dame's football team was the "Fighting Irish," and Jack was a huge fan. Ronald worried that his father would start drinking during the celebration, but Jack stayed sober. And when Ronald looked over at Jack during a banquet after the premiere, he saw the happiest expression he had ever seen on his father's face. Ronald still had mixed feelings about his father—he was ashamed of his alcoholism and yet loved him. He also hated that he couldn't be more tolerant of Jack's sickness. At Notre Dame, he felt they had grown closer. A year later, on May 18, 1941, Jack had another heart attack, and he died in the house Ronald had given him. Later, Nelle told Ronald that Jack had once said to her that the trip to Notre Dame meant a lot to him. "I was there," he told her, "when our son became a star."

While Ronald was very upset over his father's death, he had a new life to watch over. Five months earlier, on January 4, 1941, Jane had given birth to a daughter, Maureen Elizabeth Reagan. "Mermie," as she was soon called, would later remember her early childhood growing up in a Hollywood home, going to watch one of her parents film a movie, seeing pictures of all three of them in magazines, and eating dinner at the Brown Derby with her parents. She remembered her father telling her endless stories—usually silly ones—and singing her to sleep at night. But even with a baby, Jane and Ronald did not slow down their careers. Maureen spent much of her time being cared for by a nanny.

Not long after Maureen was born, the family moved into a new house in Beverly Hills. It had big picture windows that looked out toward the Pacific Ocean in the distance. The house had a pool out back, so Ronald could swim. Some of his friends from the studio would come over and hang out around the pool before dinner, including Bill and Ardis Holden, George Burns and Gracie Allen, and Jack Benny and Mary Livingstone. Neil and Bess would come over, too, and guests remember Neil and Ronald getting into endless discussions about politics. Unlike many of his acting friends, Ronald was very interested in politics, and still a big fan of President Roosevelt. Neil's politics had changed—he was now a Republican and believed Roosevelt was expanding government too much. The brothers would argue so long sometimes that other guests gave up and went inside.

Ronald's performance as George Gipp earned him more challenging roles in 1941. Warner Bros.

Ronald signs autographs for his fans through a barbed-wire fence, circa 1940.

gave him a new contract for seven years and one million dollars. He had become a bona fide star.

But Ronald's moviemaking was soon interrupted. Much of the world had been at war since 1939—Germany had conquered most of Europe. Japan was swallowing up other nations in Asia. America had been sending weapons to the British to help them fight Germany. And on December 7, 1941, Japanese forces bombed the American fleet at Pearl Harbor in Hawaii. America was going to war, and everyone needed to contribute to the effort—even actors.

FOUR

WORLD WAR II was the deadliest conflict in human history—more than sixty million people died, many of them civilians. In the United States, the war meant devoting all resources to winning. About 20 percent of American men were drafted into the armed forces, and women had to fill many jobs in factories. Those factories stopped making things like cars and made tanks instead. Basic items like food and gas were rationed.

Ronald had been a cavalry reserve officer for years—he joined so he could ride army horses on a Des Moines base. The army began assigning such officers to active duty before the war even started, preparing for the possibility of combat. Reagan was called up twice in 1941 and once in early 1942 but received deferments because the military considered the film industry important for maintaining the country's morale. But in April 1942, the army decided it needed every man possible, and Ronald was ordered to Fort Mason in San Francisco. It quickly became apparent, however, that he was not going to see combat, mostly because he wouldn't have been able to see it. An army vision test showed how nearsighted he was. One doctor told Ronald that if they sent him into battle, he might shoot at one of his own generals. Another doctor responded, "Yes, and you'd miss him."

Ronald spent five weeks in San Francisco supervising the loading of military transport ships. Then he was sent back to Los Angeles. The army had decided that movies could be useful, and Ronald was assigned to the First Motion Picture Unit, based at an old film studio. Staffed with actors, directors, and others from the studios who had been drafted, they started making movies for the army. Some were recruiting pictures, urging young men to enlist. Others were instructional films, teaching soldiers. One film Ronald starred in taught air force gunners how to identify Japanese fighter planes. Another, narrated by Ronald, showed models of Tokyo, identifying targets for plane crews so they would know what to bomb when flying over the real city.

Ronald's life in the army was not as tough as the

lives of the young men sent into combat. He was usually able to go home on weekends to see Jane and Maureen. But he was contributing to the war effort, and considering his eyesight, it was probably the best option for him. He was proud of what he did, but while he was working for the army, his contract was on hold, and his army salary was much smaller. Jane became the primary earner in the family. That family grew larger on March 18, 1945, when Michael Edward Reagan was born. Michael was adopted, since Maureen's birth had been difficult for Jane. Michael's biological mother was single and not ready to raise a child. With the help of the nanny—and Ronald on weekends—Jane raised their two kids and made several films a year.

The war had a powerful effect on Ronald's political beliefs. Once he had been a pacifist, against all wars. But as Germany and Japan began invading their neighbors, he changed his mind and decided that some wars were necessary. He believed that democratic America was a force for good in the world, and that totalitarian governments were evil. But even as the United States and its allies pushed back German and Japanese forces, seeds were being planted for a new war. One of America's allies was not a democracy—the Soviet Union, the former Russian Empire, was ruled by Joseph Stalin and a Communist government.

Communism is a philosophy from the nineteenth century that argues for a classless society. Communists believe capitalism is flawed because business owners exploit their workers. They want a society where all people share property, such as land and businesses. In practice, Stalin's government owned most property. Instead of farmers owning their land, the government took it and divided it up into large "industrial" farms, and all the people were simply workers. The government told factory managers which products to make, based on what the government thought people needed most.

The United States and the Soviet Union became allies because both opposed the Nazis, but as their armies successfully pushed toward Germany from opposite sides of Europe, and FDR, Stalin, and British Prime Minister Winston Churchill began meeting to discuss what postwar Europe would look like, their goals began to differ, and tensions began to grow between them. The Soviet Union suffered enormous casualties during the war—more than twenty-six million of its citizens died. Stalin wanted resources to help his country rebuild—he called for Germany to pay reparations. He also wanted to guarantee that postwar governments in Europe would pose no danger of invading the Soviet Union again.

The United States believed the best way to ensure peace in Europe was to create democratic governments with capitalist economies. During several peace conferences, Stalin disagreed first with FDR and later with Harry Truman, who became the U.S. president after Roosevelt's death in April 1945. In August of that year, acrimony between the two nations increased after the United States used a new weapon, an atomic bomb, against Hiroshima, Japan. The bomb destroyed the entire city almost instantly, killing tens of thousands of people. Three days later, the United States dropped another atomic bomb on the city of Nagasaki, and Japan quickly surrendered.

Now Stalin feared the United States might threaten the Soviets with their new nuclear weapon. Soviet troops occupied the eastern portion of Germany and almost all of Eastern Europe. American, British, and French troops were in most of Western Europe. Even though America and its allies wanted to create democracies in countries like Poland, Czechoslovakia, and Hungary, they could not unless they dislodged the

Soviet Army by force. In the countries he controlled, Stalin eventually established communist governments that reported to him. America established democracies in the areas it controlled. Germany was divided into four zones—three occupied by the United States, Britain, and France, which were eventually reunified into the democratic nation of West Germany, and a fourth portion, which became the Communist East Germany. The old German capital of Berlin, which was in the middle of what was now East Germany, was also divided into four parts. Three were unified to become West Berlin, an island of West Germany inside East Germany.

Ronald was discharged from the army in July 1945. He happily returned to making movies at Warner Bros. and spending nights with his family. But during the three years Ronald had served in the army, film audiences had grown fond of new stars. Warner Bros. began casting Ronald in movies he didn't want to do, usually romantic comedies. He would have preferred dramas and Westerns. He was still riding horses during his free time and loved the idea of playing a cowboy. Not long after the war, he bought a ranch in the San

Fernando Valley, about twenty miles north of his house, and several horses.

Ronald was also busy with work for the Screen Actors Guild, or SAG, a labor union that protected the rights of actors in Hollywood, particularly less famous actors who didn't have big contracts. Ronald had joined the union almost immediately after he began making films, and in 1941 he had taken a seat on the board. He enjoyed the political give-and-take of the organization—meeting with members, negotiating with studio heads, and giving speeches. After the war, convinced that liberal Americans needed to be politically active and speak out against any recurrence of fascism, he joined several political organizations— idealistic groups like the World Federalists and the Hollywood Independent Citizens Committee of the Arts, Sciences and Professions (HICCASP). Some local Democrats even asked him in 1946 if he would be interested in running for Congress. He declined—his day job was acting.

When Ronald and his brother used to argue about politics, Neil would accuse Ronald of supporting communist ideas. This upset Ronald—conservatives often unfairly accused liberals of secretly believing

ABC radio announcer Ted Malone interviews Ronald and Jane over breakfast, with Maureen sitting at the table, January 1946.

in communism. Back during the Great Depression, when capitalism appeared to be failing and people were desperate for an answer to their problems, some people in America had considered communism. A few even joined the Communist Party of the United States. But most quit the party in the late 1930s when Stalin's government became increasingly repressive.

Americans grew frightened of communism after World War II as the United States and the Soviet Union became locked in a new war of ideologies. The Cold War was the name of this growing political battle, and, simply put, the two nations were each struggling to become the most powerful country in the world. The Soviet Union wanted communism to be adopted by other countries around the world—one of communism's tenets was that a Communist revolution in one country would lead to revolutions in others. For the next forty years, the United States and the Soviet Union would not fight an actual war, but they would fight a cold war, using economics, diplomacy, espionage, and propaganda against each other.

As the Cold War intensified, many Americans feared the Communist Party of the United States was secretly taking orders from the Soviet Union to spread revolutionary ideas. They were partially right. Though many American communists did not belong to the party and did not support the Soviets, the party leaders received money and orders from Moscow. People became paranoid and demanded that the government protect them from this potential threat. One of their fears was that communists wanted to control Hollywood and what appeared on-screen.

During this period of fear, the SAG board asked Ronald to help mediate a dispute between two other unions—the Conference of Studio Unions (CSU) and the International Alliance of Theatrical Stage Employees (IATSE), which were both trying to represent people who worked behind the scenes at the studios. A year earlier, the CSU had begun a series of strikes, calling for better contracts for the set decorators. Labor disagreements and strikes continued on and off for another year.

CSU leader Herb Sorrell appealed to SAG to have actors strike as well. Sorrell had often been accused of being a communist, a charge he denied. Ronald tried to negotiate a solution with him but had no luck. In the end, Ronald and the other SAG leaders declared the strike illegitimate and said the actors should keep working.

Sorrell was angry and urged people to boycott Ronald's movies. Workers fought in front of the studios, trying to prevent the actors from going to work. While Ronald was on a movie set outside of town, someone called the studio phone and asked to speak with him. When he picked up the phone, they told him if he didn't support the strike, someone would make sure his face was never seen in pictures again. Ronald reported the threat to the police and began to carry a gun. But without SAG's support, the CSU soon collapsed. SAG's members supported Ronald's decision not to strike, and in 1947, they elected him union president. He quickly earned a reputation for being a smart leader who was effective when negotiating with the studio bosses. He would remain president through 1953.

One night in April 1947, there was a knock at Ronald's door. It was two men from the FBI, wanting to know if Ronald and Jane would tell the FBI of any communist activity by people in the film industry. Ronald and Jane agreed. He didn't give much information to the FBI—only because he didn't have much proof to give them. But he was becoming increasingly suspicious that communists were trying to take over the film industry—and America—through trickery, and he believed it was his patriotic duty to help stop them. He began speaking out against communism in his appearances at civic groups and at SAG meetings.

He also began to worry about the political groups he had joined. Unknown to him, some communist party members were joining groups like HICCASP in hope of slowly persuading liberal Americans to turn to communism. Neil had warned him of this, but Ronald had always dismissed his fears. Now Ronald realized what these communists were up to, and he quit. He began to see this as a moral issue: democracy and America were good; communism and the Soviet Union were evil. "Now I knew from firsthand experience how communists used lies, deceit, violence, or any other tactic that suited them to advance the cause of Soviet expansion," he later wrote. "I knew that America faced no more insidious or evil threat than that of communism."

In October, Ronald was called to Washington, D.C., to testify as SAG president before the House Un-American Activities Committee (HUAC), a panel of congressmen investigating whether communists were working in the government and the entertainment industry. They suspected that communists in Hollywood were secretly inserting ideas and messages into movies. They were asking, and sometimes subpoenaing, people from the industry to testify. But the committee's members seemed more interested in publicity for themselves than in fighting communism. They repeated rumors and wild accusations, hoping to scare the public. Ronald was asked whether he thought any SAG members were communists. He responded that he had suspicions about some people, but he didn't know for sure, and he wouldn't name names. Ronald hated communism but he wasn't going to smear people. Media reports called his testimony thoughtful and restrained.

The committee members were imagining a much larger communist conspiracy than actually existed, but movie studio leaders worried that the public would stop going to films—and their studios would lose money—if people thought Hollywood was full of communists. So they named ten writers who failed to cooperate with HUAC and declared they would not work in movies again. The writers were blacklisted. Soon other writers, and actors, directors, and producers—some of whom were communists, many of whom were merely suspected of being communists—were blacklisted. "Many fine people were accused wrongly of being communists simply because they were liberals," Ronald later wrote. "We formed an industry council to contact people who were being threatened with blacklisting and said to them: 'Look, we can't clear you, but we can help you clear yourself.'" If they publicly stated they were not communist, SAG would help get them off the blacklist. To some people, that wasn't enough, but that was as far as Ronald would go. Hundreds of entertainers were blacklisted, which ruined their careers.

☆ ☆ ☆

Back at the studio, Ronald was still frustrated by the parts he was getting, but Jane's film career was finally developing. Tired of being typecast, in 1945 she asked Warner Bros. to let her appear in a rival studio's movie, *The Lost Weekend.* It won several Academy Awards and convinced producers to offer Jane more difficult roles. Her next part, in *The Yearling,* was even more demanding and kept her away from home for a while, leaving the kids with Ronald and their nanny.

Despite Jane's hectic filming schedule and Ronald's busy life of movies and politics, everyone who knew the couple at the beginning of 1947 thought they still had the perfect Hollywood marriage. Early that year, Jane became pregnant again. Five months later, Ronald came down with viral pneumonia. He was very ill—Maureen later remembered an ambulance coming to the house and her father being wheeled out on a stretcher. While he was in the hospital, Ronald kept growing weaker. Jane and the rest of his family couldn't see him because the virus was highly contagious. He was close to death—he felt like he couldn't breathe. But he felt a nurse take his hand and urge him to keep breathing. He would later write that he kept breathing out of courtesy to her. Jane grew ever more upset, but soon she was in a hospital bed, too—she went into labor early. On June 26, 1947, she gave birth to a baby girl who was four months premature. The baby died the next day. Jane was shattered, and Ronald could not even see her because he was too sick. He was horribly upset, trapped in a hospital bed and unable to comfort his wife.

By the time both had recovered, they were literally in different places. Jane immediately began filming a new movie called *Johnny Belinda*, in which she played a woman who was deaf and mute, an incredibly demanding role. She hoped plunging herself into work would help her get past the pain of losing a child. Ronald was busy with SAG business and his testimony before HUAC. Reports started appearing in gossip magazines that the Hollywood dream couple was drifting apart. On a trip to New York, Jane told a reporter, "We're through. We're finished, and it's all my fault." This was news to Ronald. He was shocked when he heard about the comment. Louella Parsons asked him what had happened. "Nothing—and everything. I think Jane takes her work too seriously." He also admitted that he might have spent too much time focusing on politics. "Perhaps

I should have let someone else save the world and have saved my own home."

Still, Ronald thought that any problems in his marriage were temporary. But sometime in early 1948, he and Jane separated. Ronald took seven-year-old Maureen for a drive one evening and tried to explain to her that Mom and Dad were not going to be living together anymore. Michael was too young to understand. Neither Ronald nor Jane would ever explain what happened or why. According to Ronald's second wife, Nancy, Ronald came home one afternoon and was greeted by Jane, who told him to get out.

Jane filed for divorce in February, claiming that Ronald spent too much time working on union issues. Jane was never as interested in politics as he was. "Finally, there was nothing in common between us, nothing to sustain our marriage," she told the court. The truth was, Ronald and Jane were very different people. And as her acting career and his political hobbies took up more of their time, they had even less in common. But Ronald was deeply hurt. He attended the Academy Awards alone and watched Jane accept an Oscar for her performance in *Johnny Belinda*. He was later seen crying at a party.

FIVE

RONALD REMAINED MISERABLE for months after his divorce. A close friend later said that he was "despondent, in a way I had never seen, because usually he was such a happy optimistic man." His film career was not going the way he wanted—Warner Bros. continued to offer him fluffy comedic parts. At night, he went home to an empty apartment—he had moved back into the same building he had lived in before he got married, bringing a desk, his books, and a stuffed lamb Maureen had given him. Jane enrolled Maureen at a nearby boarding school soon afterward and enrolled Michael a year later. But the kids came home on weekends, and their father was usually waiting, ready to take them up to his ranch. Maureen later wrote that she saw him almost as much after the divorce as before. But she also began to notice that her father, while very loving and warm, was very private, never sharing his closest feelings.

Ronald withdrew into his shell for a time—he dated some, but not seriously. He kept busy with politics. As SAG president he began making a series of speeches in 1949 defending the values of people in the film industry. The scare over communism had left Hollywood with a bad reputation. Ronald said in his speeches that people in Hollywood shared the same values as most Americans, denouncing communism in the process.

Despite his work, he was still unhappy. But that November something happened that would change Ronald's life forever, and, as he later put it, end the emptiness inside him. A film director named Mervyn LeRoy called him up and said that one of the actresses in a movie he was directing needed the help of the SAG president. Nancy Davis was worried that people thought she was a communist because her name had shown up on communist organizations' mailing lists. She outspokenly denied being a communist, so Ronald said he would be happy to help.

Ronald quickly discovered that it was simply a case of mistaken identity—a different actress named Nancy

Davis was on those lists. But LeRoy suggested that Ronald take the young actress to dinner and tell her himself. Sensing he was being set up on a blind date, the SAG president reluctantly agreed. His suspicions were right—while Nancy's fears of being smeared were honest, when LeRoy had suggested contacting Ronald, she remembered how "nice and good looking" he was in his movies and thought he was someone she should meet. On November 15, 1949, Ronald met Nancy for dinner. She found him handsome, kind, and interesting. And being with Nancy made Ronald happy for the first time in a while. They began dating—in fact, they went out four nights in a row after that first night.

Nancy, as everyone called her, was born Anne Frances Robbins, in New York City, on July 6, 1921. Her mother was an actress, her father a car salesman. But her dad left not long after she was born. In 1929, her mother met and married a doctor, Loyal Davis, who adopted Nancy as his own daughter. After college, Nancy began acting on Broadway, and then moved to Hollywood and started appearing in films.

Despite their happy first dates, Ronald was hesitant to get involved in another serious relationship, though many of his friends felt Nancy was wonderful for him. She respected his concerns at first, because she sensed how badly his divorce had hurt him. They went out to dinner and often watched movies at his apartment. Soon he invited her to come to his ranch for the weekend—he had just bought a new ranch farther west near Lake Malibou. Nancy quickly discovered she would spend the entire weekend painting fences he had built. Eventually Maureen and Michael visited the ranch at the same time she was there.

But after almost two years together, with no sign of a ring, Nancy told Ronnie, as she called him, that her agent had a part for her in a play in New York. She asked him if she should take it. Before she could accept the role, Ronald finally asked her to marry him. Even after that he dragged his feet setting a date until finally, on March 4, 1952, he and Nancy were married in a quiet ceremony with just a minister and their friends Bill and Ardis Holden present. Ronald couldn't have delayed much longer without complications—Nancy was pregnant. And on October 21 she gave birth to a daughter, whom they named Patricia Ann—or Patti.

Newlyweds Ronald and Nancy cut their wedding cake in Toluca Lake, California, March 4, 1952.

☆ ☆ ☆

Ronald would later say, "If Nancy Davis hadn't come along when she did, I would have lost my soul." Nancy herself told a reporter, "When I say my life began with Ronnie, well, it's true. It did. I can't imagine life without him." They would be inseparable once they were married, and Ronald, so often guarded about letting anyone get too close to his heart, would let Nancy closer than anyone else.

"What is Ronald Reagan really like?" Nancy later wrote. "The secret is that there really is no secret. He is exactly the man he appears to be." Ronald never acted in real life, she said. And while he was incredibly friendly, writing endless letters to strangers who sent him fan mail, some of his closest friends were disappointed he didn't open up to them more. She believed that his childhood—the moves, Jack's alcoholism— turned Ronald into a loner. "Ronnie is an affable and gregarious man who enjoys other people, but unlike most of us, he doesn't need them for companionship or approval."

Nancy also valued the fact that while other people—herself included—grew agitated and nervous during a crisis, Ronald would stay calm and optimistic.

"But it can also be difficult to live with somebody so relentlessly upbeat. There have been times . . . when I felt Ronnie wasn't being realistic and I longed for him to show at least a little anxiety. I seem to do the worrying for both of us." Nancy would very quickly see herself as her husband's protector, the one to defend him when he refused to see the bad in situations or other people. Ronald recognized this.

While Ronald's personal life was much happier, his career was still stalled. Ronald was a good actor but not a superstar. Entering his forties, he could no longer play the young hero, but he never graduated to gritty dramatic roles that older actors got. In 1951, he costarred in a movie with a chimpanzee titled *Bedtime for Bonzo*. After that, he decided not to accept any more parts he didn't like, even if it meant appearing in fewer films and earning less money.

Luckily, he got a generous job offer in 1954. The General Electric corporation had been looking for a host for its network television program *General Electric Theater* and wanted Ronald. The company's executives thought Ronald's familiar, likeable face would draw movie fans to the relatively new medium of television.

Moreover, film actors were considered more prestigious than TV stars.

The show was thirty minutes long and ran on CBS on Sunday nights, right after the popular *Ed Sullivan Show*. Each week, Ronald introduced a new drama, usually based on a play, short story, or novel. Sometimes Ronald appeared in the drama, too, and Nancy also acted in a few episodes. The show had drawn poor ratings during its first two seasons, but just four months after Ronald joined the show, it had become one of the top ten shows on TV. It rejuvenated Ronald's career. Millions of viewers, many of whom had not seen his earlier movies, watched this friendly, dignified host each week in their living rooms.

Appearing on GE's show gave Ronald more than fame—it gave him financial security. After two years he was able to build a new house in the Palisades overlooking the Pacific Ocean. GE filled the house with all its latest electric gadgets and then filmed Ronald and Nancy showing them off during a segment for the show—it was a way for the company to encourage viewers to emulate their favorite stars.

Soon the house had two children running around—on May 20, 1958, Ronald and Nancy had a second child, a son named Ronald Prescott Reagan. Ron, as most people called him, had fond memories of growing up in the house, swimming with his dad in the big pool out back. Patti later said, "Both my brother and I learned to swim probably before we could walk."

Ronald's older children felt awkward about Patti and Ron at first, but Maureen loved Nancy and soon grew closer to her siblings. Michael began spending all his weekends with Ronald and Nancy when he was fourteen. He had been at boarding school since he was five and was struggling with a lot of problems—he was especially troubled about his adoption. He and Nancy had several fights, but at sixteen he started at a new school in Arizona, spending the weekends with Nancy's parents. There he started to do better in school and feel more confident.

As part of his job with GE, Ronald was also a spokesman for the company and spent three months of each year visiting divisions around the country. His first trips began not long after the show premiered in 1954. At first, these stops were simply tours of factories followed by short meetings with employees. Ronald would tell some stories about life in Hollywood, then take questions from the workers. Usually they asked about celebrities or what it was like working on the show. Ronald would also sometimes visit with civics groups from the local town. These events helped build public goodwill for GE. About a year after the tours started, Ronald was asked by a local teachers' group in one town to give a speech to its members—they were holding an annual gathering and needed a keynote speaker and figured a famous TV star would be fun. The GE handler who traveled with Ronald on his tours said he couldn't write a speech on short notice, but Ronald told him not to worry—he could write it himself.

The speech he gave that night was a variation of the one he had been giving for years as SAG president. At first Ronald told anecdotes about life in Hollywood, but then he became serious and spoke about the inherent virtue of democracy. He spoke of how America and its special belief in freedom were in an ideological struggle with other political philosophies, like communism, that did not value liberty. He got a standing ovation, and his handler reported back to his superiors how talented Ronald was on the stump. The executives began asking him to give speeches during his plant visits. When those went well, they asked him to give speeches to various organizations in the towns he visited.

GE executives never told Ronald what to say in his speeches. Their only rule was that he could not be partisan, endorsing political candidates or parties. It helped that most agreed with what he was saying. Ronald's speech changed regularly, but his overall theme remained the same. He would start by speaking about Hollywood and how communists had tried to "infiltrate" the film industry. He would denounce what he saw as communism's deceitful strategies around the world and then extol America's belief in freedom. Then he shifted to what he saw as a new threat to that freedom—the growing size of government. He would explain how he thought taxes were growing too large, all to feed unnecessary government programs. He warned that such expansive government was similar to communism. "I'd emphasize that we as Americans should get together and take back the liberties we were losing," he later wrote.

Ronald had been afraid of flying ever since he was on a choppy flight in 1937. During his tours for GE, he traveled by train and car. Traveling to so many towns meant that he met a lot of different people who told him about their lives and work. What stuck in his mind was how many people complained that government regulations were getting in the way of business. He began to incorporate these stories into his speech as more examples of government growing too large. He kept his speech on a set of four-by-six index cards, and as he picked up new tidbits of information or thought of new lines, he would add a card. If a story or line didn't get a good reaction, he got rid of the card. He was always perfecting it. And because he was repeatedly giving it, he could practice his delivery. "Those GE tours became an almost postgraduate course in political science for me," he later wrote.

On July 25, 1962, Nelle Reagan died. She had been in increasing pain from osteoporosis for years, and had spent the last few living in a nursing home in Los Angeles. She had also suffered from severe senility in her final years, and decades later her family would come to believe she had suffered from Alzheimer's disease. Ronald was devastated, though he never said much about his mother's death. But he firmly believed that she was reunited with Jack.

Also in 1962, GE executives decided not to renew *General Electric Theater* because its ratings had been declining. Ronald's contract ended. He had some money saved up, and after a year his brother helped get him a job. Neil was vice president of an advertising agency that represented Borax cleaner, and Borax was sponsoring a Western show called *Death Valley Days*. The host of the show was ill, and Neil suggested his brother as a replacement. Ronald especially liked the fact that on some days he could drive from his ranch to the studio and tape his part without changing out of his dusty ranch clothes.

Even though GE was no longer booking Ronald, civic groups, businesses, and other organizations kept hiring him to address their meetings. Now he was speaking for himself, and his talks grew more overtly political. He had developed a vision for America, and he wanted to share it. He also started receiving invitations from Republicans to speak at their fund-raising events. He was still a registered Democrat, but he accepted. He was rapidly realizing that his views—particularly his antipathy toward what he saw as high taxes and unnecessary government programs—were a lot closer to the Republicans' views. Ronald didn't think he had abandoned the Democrats; instead he felt the Democrats had abandoned him. He believed that while FDR had supported government programs during the crisis of the Depression, he would never have supported making such programs permanent. Democrats felt that these programs—like welfare, which financially supported poor families—were the right way to help people in trouble. Ronald thought that all welfare did was encourage people to stop working and depend on government help. Only capitalism and freedom could bring prosperity.

The same year that GE fired Ronald, former Republican Vice President Richard Nixon was running to be governor of California. Ronald contacted Nixon and offered to campaign for him. (Maureen was especially excited by this. She had inherited her father's love of politics and had been a volunteer for Nixon's presidential campaign in 1960.) Halfway through the gubernatorial campaign, as Ronald was speaking at pro-Nixon events around the state, he changed his party registration. He was now a Republican.

SIX

WHEN RONALD HAD been a young man in a Democratic household, the Republicans primarily believed in supporting businesses and keeping America out of messy foreign affairs. But the Depression and the New Deal led many Americans to support more aggressive federal intervention in the economy, and World War II and the Cold War moved most Americans away from any dreams of isolation from the rest of the world. The number of voters who identified themselves as Republicans shrank dramatically.

By 1964, Republicans were struggling to find their identity and had splintered their support between two presidential candidates, moderate New York governor Nelson Rockefeller and conservative Arizona senator

Ronald and Nancy in the pool with Ron at home on their ranch, January 1965. At the time Ronald was still swimming daily.

Barry Goldwater. Ronald fell in the Goldwater camp early on. After Goldwater defeated Rockefeller in a very close nomination battle, Goldwater asked Ronald to be his campaign co-chairman in California. From the moment Ronald switched parties, he was a Republican celebrity—conservative candidates in California and other states sought his support. Some Republicans had even approached him in 1962 and urged him to run for senator. Reading about this in a newspaper, Maureen wrote her father and told him that he should do it. He could win, she felt. He wrote back, "Mermie, I really appreciate your support, but if we're going to talk about what could be, well, I could be President—ha, ha!—but of course, that's not going to happen." While Ronald enjoyed his political role, he still thought of himself as an actor whom few people would take seriously if he decided to run for office.

The Goldwater job required Ronald to tour the state, speaking to crowds, urging people to vote or make a campaign contribution. Ronald eagerly adapted the speech he had already been giving. But the Goldwater campaign struggled. President Lyndon Johnson's social programs—the very programs Ronald thought were wasteful—were fairly popular. What's more, Johnson was able to paint Goldwater as a conservative extremist who would be dangerous in the Oval Office. His campaign even made an ad suggesting Goldwater would start a nuclear war. The senator didn't help himself—Goldwater had a habit of saying controversial things.

Late in the summer of 1964, Ronald gave a speech at a Hollywood nightclub to a crowd of wealthy donors who each gave one thousand dollars to Goldwater's campaign. Holmes Tuttle, a local businessman who owned a chain of car dealerships and had organized the dinner, chatted with Ronald afterward. To Tuttle and the other Los Angeles businessmen at his table, Ronald was a better spokesman for Goldwater than the senator himself. The men proposed to Ronald that they buy some airtime on national television so Ronald could give his speech to a national audience. Ronald eagerly agreed.

The televised address, which aired on October 27, 1964, was called "A Time for Choosing." In it, Ronald laid out his vision—that America was a special place, a beacon to the world, because it valued individual freedom above all else. But that liberty must be maintained, and Goldwater was the man to do it: "It's time we asked ourselves if we still know the freedoms intended for us by the Founding Fathers. This idea that government was beholden to the people, that it had no other source of power except the sovereign people, is still the newest, most unique idea in all the long history of man's relation to man." He warned that growing taxes and federal aid programs were leading America toward socialism, that if Americans didn't restrict their government, it would restrict them.

People watching Ronald found him positive, warm, and encouraging. The speech raised one million dollars for the Goldwater campaign in just a few days. Goldwater lost the election a week later, however, receiving just 38.4 percent of the vote.

Two months after the election, Tuttle gathered several friends, most of whom were self-made millionaires. They called themselves "Friends of Ronald Reagan" and they believed Ronald was the best hope for the GOP's future. They went to ask him to run for governor of California.

Ronald's response was clear. "I can't remember my

exact words, but I said, in effect: 'You're out of your mind.'" Ronald was ambitious, but he was also proud. He worried that if he tried to run for office, he would fall flat on his face. Deep down, he wanted to run—but he also wanted to know that other people really wanted him to run, too.

Tuttle and his friends convinced Ronald to let them begin putting together a campaign team to prove to him that mounting a serious run for governor was possible. And soon, letters were pouring in from California voters who wanted him to run. Nancy later wrote, "For about two weeks we talked about it constantly—during dinner, after dinner, and late at night in bed. After the Goldwater defeat, with the party in shambles, Ronnie felt he could play a role in helping to put it back together. Pretty soon I just knew that he'd eventually say yes." Still playing it safe, Ronald began an exploratory campaign, touring the state, introducing himself to voters and answering their questions, while the Friends of Ronald Reagan raised money and assembled the full campaign staff. Before long, Ronald knew he was going to do it. He let his campaign managers know he was serious when he told them he was willing to fly to campaign events, despite his fear of planes. He was in.

In 1966, the year Ronald hit the campaign trail, there were more than 250,000 U.S. soldiers in South Vietnam, helping South Vietnamese forces fight communists from North Vietnam. What had looked like a simple mission of the United States providing aid to stem the spread of communism had turned into an undeclared American war. Thousands of U.S. citizens took to the streets to protest.

At the same time, the Civil Rights Movement continued to make progress in pushing for equality, but tensions were growing. Black Americans were frustrated by the slow pace of the reforms and by the racism and poverty they confronted every day.

California had its own issues. In 1964, students at the University of California–Berkeley had protested after the school stopped allowing them to hand out leaflets. Peaceful demonstrations led to stronger action, and eventually a group occupied a school administration building until police forcibly dragged them out. A year later, riots broke out in the poor black neighborhood of Watts in Los Angeles when a simple traffic arrest turned violent. After six days of havoc, thirty-four people were dead, more than one thousand wounded, and hundreds of buildings damaged.

With Californians losing confidence in their government, it was the right time for an outsider like Ronald to run. The incumbent governor, Pat Brown, seemed to be struggling to control the state, and to make matters worse, in 1966 he was confronting a huge budget shortfall. Not eager to raise taxes in an election year, Brown came up with an accounting gimmick—he used the money the state was collecting for 1967 and spent it on the 1966 budget instead. He thought it was better than raising taxes, but voters saw it as a dirty trick.

No actor had ever been governor, however, and many Californians questioned whether Ronald could handle the job. Brown knew this and loved to say that while he had been working in government, Ronald had been filming *Bedtime for Bonzo*. But while Ronald had never served in government, he had more political experience than people realized. His work as SAG president and all those speeches he gave for

GE had been practice for campaigning. His campaign managers were quickly impressed with Ronald's natural, friendly appearances in front of crowds. He could think on his feet when asked tough questions. When people wanted to know why he thought an actor with no political experience could be governor, he replied, "Sure, the man who has the job has more experience than anyone else—that's why I'm running." At a time when career politicians like Brown seemed to be having a hard time controlling the country, this was an appealing answer.

Ronald was also educated on political issues and had a strong set of beliefs—an asset for a candidate. Unfortunately, all his knowledge concerned national issues—he knew nothing about California state government. He didn't even know what his job as governor would entail if he won. So the campaign staff asked Ronald to meet with outside experts for a series of study sessions. First he met with Charles Conrad, who had been in the state assembly for almost a decade and was willing to explain the basics of the state government to Ronald, like how laws were passed and what the governor's responsibilities were.

His staff also brought in a team of behavioral psychologists that analyzed Ronald's speeches and interviewed him about his political philosophy. They used the information to decide what his platform should be, and then compiled a set of briefing books to educate Ronald on the issues and his platform. He soaked up the data and began using it in his speeches.

"Once I got on the campaign trail," Ronald later wrote, "I discovered, a little to my surprise, that I enjoyed campaigning." Nancy, however, made it clear to Ronald's advisers that she did not want to give speeches. Even though she had been an actress, she found the idea of being just herself in front of a crowd frightening. But as Ronald kept up an exhausting pace, flying around the state to multiple events each day, they asked her if she wouldn't mind doing some question-and-answer sessions with crowds. She agreed and soon found it wasn't so bad.

In June, Reagan won the Republican primary with 65 percent of the vote. Brown's attacks on Ronald's acting career grew stronger after that, which bothered Ronald. It wasn't necessarily that people thought an actor couldn't be a politician—he was content to try and disprove that. What bugged him was that Brown and others kept insulting the quality of his movies, calling him a "B-movie actor." Ronald was proud of his days as an actor. But for the sake of the campaign, he held back any retorts and focused on stressing what he would do as governor.

And Ronald seemed like a competent candidate to voters. In a September TV debate, Ronald was calm and intelligent while Brown looked tired and hostile. And on election night in early November, the results showed that the people of California were going to give the actor a chance. Reagan won, with 58 percent of the vote.

SEVEN

"AS FUNNY AS it might seem now, when I gave in to the appeals to run for governor, I had never given much thought to the possibility I might win," Ronald Reagan wrote years later. His campaign press secretary Lyn Nofziger put it another way, "We were amateurs." When he did win, Reagan and his staff realized they had less than two months to come up with a plan. Running for office as a critic of the government was very different from leading a government.

The job also meant a lot of changes for Reagan and his family. On election night, Maureen, Michael, and Ron were by his side when the returns came in. Patti was at boarding school in Arizona, and when she learned he had won, she called him and cried into the phone, "How could you do this to me?" She was

The Reagans celebrate Ronald's victory in California's governor race at the Biltmore Hotel in Los Angeles, California, November 8, 1966.

fourteen years old and identified a lot more with pro-testing students at Berkeley than with a Republican governor. But while Patti stayed at school pouting, Nancy, eight-year-old Ron, and the new governor packed their belongings and moved almost four hundred miles north to Sacramento, the state capital. Reagan kept his house in the Pacific Palisades—the family would sometimes fly home for weekends—but he sold his ranch. The governor's salary was a lot smaller than a TV star's, and he couldn't afford to keep the property.

On January 2, 1967, just a few minutes after midnight at the state's capitol, Reagan put his hand on a Bible and took the oath of office while his family and guests looked on. In his inaugural address, he promised to reform California's welfare system, to restore law and order, especially on university campuses, but most of all, to bring fiscal discipline back to the government by cutting spending. "We are going to squeeze and cut and trim until we reduce the cost of government," he said. "For many years now, you and I have been shushed like children and told there are no simple answers to the complex problems beyond our comprehension. Well, the truth is, there are simple answers—there are just not easy ones."

Reagan couldn't afford to get off to a slow start—he was already facing a crisis before he even took office. Brown's accounting gimmick with the state budget left a $460 million deficit, and California's constitution required the state government to enact a balanced budget by June 30. A budget proposal had to be submitted to the legislature not long after the inauguration.

Reagan's biggest challenge in tackling the deficit was working with the members of the state senate and state assembly who were career politicians and skeptical of an actor. It wouldn't help that both chambers were controlled by Democrats. Facing a hostile legislature, most governors would try to court members, but Reagan didn't like socializing with politicians at dinners or cocktail parties. He had never been much of a partier, preferring the company of close friends or his family. In Sacramento, he liked to leave his office by six P.M., head home to exercise, eat dinner with Nancy, and watch TV or read briefings and newspapers. So Reagan's staff usually talked with legislators, and if they couldn't win support for his ideas, Reagan followed FDR's example and gave TV or radio speeches to the people, calling for their support.

Not courting lawmakers directly would make it harder to get his budget enacted. And when he released his proposal, it received poor reviews. He called for a 10 percent cut of every government department. That was impractical—different departments had different funding needs. Some of his proposed cuts—to the state university system and the state mental health system—triggered outraged reactions from legislators and the media.

In the end, Reagan resolved the deficit by being a pragmatist. First, he dropped the proposed cuts people objected to. Then he sat down with Assembly Speaker Jesse Unruh, the Democrats' leader, to bargain. "I realized after a while that to accomplish what I wanted, I'd have to do some negotiating with them," he later wrote. He wanted to find a solution. "When I began entering into the give and take of legislative bargaining," he later wrote, "a lot of the most radical conservatives who supported me during the election didn't like it. 'Compromise' was a dirty word to them. They wanted it all or nothing. I'd learned while negotiating union contracts that you seldom got everything you asked for."

The passed budget did not completely erase the deficit, however, and Reagan realized he would have to raise taxes. He had been railing against tax increases for two decades but saw no other solution for the deficit that he and the legislature could agree on. Reagan also knew that this might be the last time he could raise taxes without a voter outcry. The deficit was Brown's fault. Unruh and Reagan agreed on a $1 billion tax increase. Reagan did not find the solution ideal, but he explained his decision to voters, and as the governor predicted, they blamed Brown.

Because of the tax increase, California's government was flush with revenues for the rest of Reagan's time in office. Eventually, Reagan was able to make tax cuts and give the people refunds when the state had surplus money. He also earned a reputation with many legislators as a reasonable man who was willing to compromise.

Overall, Reagan found his first year in office stressful and sometimes wondered if he'd made the right choice leaving acting. Every day his staff seemed to discover a new problem. He said in a speech that he was undergoing on-the-job training. "When I got to Sacramento, I felt like an Egyptian tank driver reading a set of Russian instructions." One day he felt a sharp pain in his stomach that wouldn't go away. Doctors told him he had an ulcer, probably caused by stress. He began watching what he ate and taking medicine.

He also felt like the media was constantly attacking him. "In Hollywood, Nancy and I had become used to having critics take shots at us and reading things about ourselves in the papers that weren't true," he wrote. "But what we found in Sacramento made our Hollywood experience seem mild by comparison." Reagan enjoyed high ratings after his first year in office, and the media wasn't that hard on him compared to other politicians, but he never got used to the criticism.

And Nancy grew increasingly concerned that someone might physically attack her husband. One night, she and Reagan were in bed when they heard a loud bang. They both jumped out of bed, and a security agent assigned to protect them came in and told them to stay away from any windows. Police had seen two men under the couple's bedroom window, trying to light a Molotov cocktail. An officer fired a shot at the men (the loud bang they had heard), but they got away.

After about a year Reagan adjusted to his job. He learned to socialize with lawmakers, inviting them over for a drink and for regular parties at his house. "I also discovered the value of picking up a telephone and calling a legislator to tell him or her why I thought he or she should vote for something I wanted." One day he reached for his stomach medicine but then put it down. He no longer felt any pain, and his doctors confirmed that the ulcer was gone.

Governor Reagan enjoyed high popularity ratings in California, and nationally he was a hero to conservative Republicans. Ever since his 1964 speech in support of Goldwater, conservatives had seen him as an ideal candidate for president. The leading Republican contenders in 1968 were Nelson Rockefeller and former vice president Richard Nixon. Many conservatives thought Rockefeller was too moderate and worried that Nixon could not win. They began urging Reagan to run. But he wasn't sure he was ready. "I'd been governor for less than two years and I said it would look ridiculous if I ran for president," he later wrote. "Clearly [he was] ambitious," Press Secretary Lyn Nofziger later said. "But he didn't want to embarrass himself. He was a very careful guy." One of his advisers, Tom Reed, and Nofziger were urging Republicans around the country to "draft" Reagan to run, by putting him on GOP primary ballots and voting for him. And Reagan encouraged this with his remarks. At his weekly press conferences, reporters would ask if he was running and he would say no, but he also said if the people wanted him to run, he would.

In the spring, California party leaders approached Reagan and asked if they could place his name on the state's presidential primary ballot. Reagan agreed, and he won the primary that June. He also won a few other delegates in state primaries where supporters who wanted him to run had put his name on the ballot.

By the time he arrived at the Republican convention in Miami in August, Reagan and his team were discussing the possibility that he could win the nomination. But Nixon worked aggressively to make sure he had enough loyal delegates. On the first ballot, Nixon won 697 votes, 30 more than he needed. Reagan came in third with 182 and quickly threw his support behind Nixon. He later wrote that he was relieved when he didn't get the nomination. He felt it was too soon.

Reagan was serving as governor at a time when young people, especially college students, were questioning America's values more than ever before. Coming from a generation that had endured the hardships of the Depression and World War II, Reagan had a difficult time understanding the complaints of these kids—and he didn't make much of an effort, either. Early in his first term, a delegation of California university students asked to meet with him. "When the delegation arrived in the capitol, some were barefoot and several were wearing torn T-shirts," he later wrote. "Their spokesman began, 'Governor, we want to talk to you, but I think you should realize that it's impossible for you to understand us. You weren't raised in a time of satellites or computers. You didn't live in an age of space travel . . .' While he paused to take a breath, I said, 'You're absolutely right. We didn't have those things when we were your age. We invented them.'"

California was a main birthplace of youth movements. U.C. Berkeley had been a hotbed of protest since 1964. Later in the sixties, student protests became common throughout the nation as large portions of the American public turned against the Vietnam War. And as young people began questioning the government's war policy, they began questioning everything about American society. Some called for equal rights for women and minorities. Some experimented with drugs like marijuana and LSD. Some just dropped out of school and gave up on trying to get a job. The hippie movement began in San Francisco in 1965.

When Reagan gave speeches, he often joked, "We have some hippies in California. For those of you who don't know what a hippie is, he's a fellow who dresses like Tarzan, has hair like Jane, and smells like Cheetah." It always got a big laugh from his older, conservative audiences. When he visited campuses, he was often greeted by demonstrating students. At one school, hundreds of students stood in silent protest as Reagan walked from his car to a building. He walked past them all, then turned as he got to the door, put a finger to his lips and said, "Shhhhhhhhhhh!" The students all began laughing.

Reagan tried to leave campus protests to university administrators to handle. But in January 1969, several arson and fire-bombing attempts were made on the Berkeley campus, and in early February, students trying to get to class were attacked by demonstrating students and other activists. Reagan sent in the California Highway Patrol to restore order, but isolated violent incidents kept occurring. On May 15 a full riot broke out. The protesters threw rocks and bottles at the advancing police. The police responded with tear gas and, finally, shotguns. A young man was hit by a gun blast and killed. Sixty other people were wounded. The police appealed to Reagan for help, and he sent National Guard soldiers to the campus. Martial law was enforced for more than two weeks. After that, the campus settled down.

Reagan never doubted his decision to send in soldiers. He believed that the demonstrators were breaking the law. They reminded him of the striking CSU workers and communists in Hollywood he believed were trying to damage America by destroying its values. He never listened to the student protesters' point of view, and when they resorted to violence, he did everything he could to stop them.

☆ ☆ ☆

"By the end of 1969, I realized I was going to need more time than I had left in my first term to accomplish my goals," Reagan later wrote. "And I'd had enough experience—and enjoyment—at it to know I didn't want to stop." Reagan had learned a lot in his first three years in office. The actor was now an effective politician. In the 1970 campaign, he easily won reelection with 52.9 percent of the vote.

Reagan's top priority in his second term was welfare reform. Welfare, or Aid to Families with Dependent Children (AFDC), was a government program that sent financial aid to poor families with children. FDR's administration had created the program in 1935 during the Depression. The federal government provided some of the aid money; the states provided the rest and set the rules on who was eligible for benefits and how much they received. In 1963, 375,000 people received benefits in California. By the time Reagan began his second term, welfare rolls had swelled to more than 1.5 million. Republicans believed some people were taking advantage of the system, collecting benefits they weren't entitled to.

Reagan proposed more than seventy changes to the state system to try to keep people from abusing welfare. Meanwhile the Democrats argued that welfare recipients didn't receive enough money. The state had not increased benefit payments since 1957, and inflation meant that those payments weren't worth as much. In 1971, an average family of three in San Francisco needed $271 a month for basic needs. The welfare benefit for such a family was $172. The Democrats accused Reagan of not caring about poor people.

"I have never questioned the need to take care of people who, through no fault of their own, can't provide for themselves," Reagan later wrote. "But I am against open-ended welfare programs that invite generation after generation of potentially productive people to remain on the dole. Welfare was taking away the very thing that people needed most—the initiative to provide for themselves." Reagan was never heartless about the poor—he often gave to charities. But he believed government welfare was bad, and he usually focused on the people who had well-paid jobs but were illegally receiving checks, rather than on the families who accepted government aid because they had nowhere else to turn.

The Democrats kept Reagan's welfare proposal bottled up in committee for months. So the governor appealed to the people, explaining his plan and asking them to send letters to assembly members. Thousands of voters wrote. The new assembly speaker, Democrat Bob Moretti, reached out to Reagan and told him any reform would require the two of them to compromise. Reagan said he was happy to negotiate. For eleven days, the two men and their staff members negotiated, crafting a bill they could both support. Reagan got tougher rules on who got benefits—administrators were required to thoroughly check for fraud, and assets were counted more carefully to make sure a family was truly needy. Moretti got increases in benefits for those who deserved them—80 percent of those left on the rolls received a cost-of-living increase. California's law became a model for future welfare-reform efforts.

Reagan's other major priority for his second term was cutting taxes, especially property taxes, which had grown much larger in the past decade. Democrats continued to oppose many of his efforts, but thanks to his strong relationship with Moretti, he passed a bill in

1972 granting $780 million in property-tax relief and improving funding to public schools.

Reagan left office at the end of 1974 with a solid record as governor. It was not the conservative revolution he had promised—government revenues and size had not shrunk. But Reagan had halted the government's growth.

Holmes Tuttle urged Reagan to run for a third term, but Reagan declined. He was considering national possibilities and, for the time being, wanted to relax. He and Nancy had purchased a new ranch in Santa Barbara that year, and he was looking forward to some time to himself.

EIGHT

IN JANUARY 1975, Reagan moved back to his house in the Pacific Palisades with Nancy and Ron. Reagan's favorite place to spend time, however, was on their seven-hundred-acre ranch in the Santa Ynez Mountains north of Santa Barbara. He named it Rancho del Cielo, or ranch of the sky, because to reach it you had to drive up a road that was often covered by low clouds. All that stood on the land was a simple adobe house, barely fit to live in. With the help of two former staffers from Sacramento, Reagan began to fix up the property, expanding the house and fencing pastures for his horses. "His form of relaxation was very hard physical labor," Dennis LeBlanc, Reagan's ranch manager, later told an interviewer.

Reagan also loved to just ride the trails. Nancy

sometimes rode with him, but often he went alone. "He would go out for hours at a time," Ron later said. "He'd just sort of disappear into the hills." After all these years, Reagan was still a loner. He and Nancy saw friends in Los Angeles, but he was just as happy alone at the ranch. Most friends would always say they never felt they knew the real Reagan. And while all his children describe him as a loving and kind father, they never felt they could fully confide in him. Michael would later say his father was "the only adult male I ever trusted." But he also said, "He just finds it difficult to hug his own children." Patti once told a reporter, "I never knew who he was; I could never get through to him." Ron said, "I knew him as well as anybody, outside my mother. But still, there is something that he holds back. You get just so far, and then the curtain drops, and you don't go any further."

Despite spending so much time at the ranch, Reagan didn't drop out of politics completely. He resumed giving speeches to various groups around the country, delivering eight to ten every month and earning a nice fee for each one. Two of his former aides, Mike Deaver and Peter Hannaford, opened an office and supervised his speaking schedule. They also kept him in the me-

The Reagan family in front of their home in Pacific Palisades, California. From left to right: Patti, Nancy, Ronald, Michael, Maureen, and Ron, with Pogo lying at their feet, 1976.

dia—Reagan began writing a weekly column (with a staffer's help) that appeared in 174 newspapers, and he gave a weekly radio address (which he wrote himself) that was broadcast by 200 different stations. All of these pursuits kept Reagan fresh in the minds of conservative voters, and it provided a steady, generous income. "For Ronnie, this was the perfect job," Nancy later wrote. "He could earn a good living by doing what he enjoyed—communicating his beliefs about the direction in which the country ought to move." Nancy enjoyed it, too—she did not miss public life.

But Reagan wasn't planning to remain a political commentator forever. Conservatives from around the country were urging him to run for president, and unlike in 1968, he no longer thought he was too inexperienced. "I didn't automatically turn a deaf ear to the appeals," he later wrote. "I had changed, probably because when I'd been governor I'd felt the excitement and satisfaction that comes from being able to bring about change, not just talk about it."

When Nixon won the presidency in 1968, Reagan and his advisers expected that Nixon might serve two terms and Reagan could compete for the nomination in a wide-open field in 1976. But that changed the summer of 1974. Nixon resigned that August, to avoid facing possible impeachment by Congress over his role in the Watergate scandal. During the 1972 Nixon reelection campaign, burglars hired by the White House had broken into the Democratic campaign headquarters in the

Watergate hotel to install eavesdropping equipment. Investigations into the break-in revealed Nixon's two-year effort to cover up White House involvement, plus several other dirty deeds by his administration. Vice President Gerald Ford took over as president.

By the time Reagan was out of the governor's office, Ford was committed to running in 1976. This presented Reagan with a difficult dilemma. On the one hand, the GOP was so weakened by Watergate that party leaders were urging everyone to unite behind Ford. If Reagan challenged Ford in the primaries, he could be accused of disloyalty. On the other hand, Ford's popularity had plummeted after he pardoned Nixon. A Democrat might beat him even if no one challenged him.

Reagan approached the decision with his usual caution. "This was frustrating for his friends and supporters," Nancy later wrote. "But whenever Ronnie is faced with a major decision he moves deliberately. I had found that out for myself more than twenty years earlier, when it took him forever to consider running for another office—the husband of Nancy Davis." Meanwhile, his allies were preparing in case Reagan decided to run.

In July of 1975, a week after Ford formally announced he would run, Reagan's supporters formed Citizens for Reagan, an exploratory committee devoted to seeing if there was sufficient support for Reagan. Most of Reagan's friends and staff from previous campaigns were helping—Deaver, Ed Meese, Lyn Nofziger, Holmes Tuttle. Reagan and his advisers were worried that no one on the team had much national campaign experience, so they hired John Sears—a young, talented Washington lawyer who had helped Nixon win in '68—to be manager. Sears thought Ford had no support among Republican voters—he told Reagan that if he challenged Ford and beat him in an early primary state like New Hampshire, Ford's campaign would collapse.

On Halloween, Reagan asked his three adult children to come to the house and join Nancy and seventeen-year-old Ron. He had an announcement. Maureen, who had been working on TV as a news reporter and occasionally as an actress, lived nearby and was there soon. Michael and his fiancée, Colleen (they were to get married a month later), drove up from Orange County—after years of avoiding his father's political career, Michael was growing more interested. He was also gaining confidence—he had discovered a passion for speedboat racing and was quite good at it. But Patti didn't come. Since dropping out of college, she had moved in with a guitarist in the Eagles rock band and wasn't talking to her parents.

As they gathered in the living room, Reagan said he was going to run for president. He told his family, "I've been speaking out on the issues for quite a while now, and it's time to put myself on the line. In three weeks I'm going to announce that I'm entering the race. Otherwise, I'd feel like the guy who always sat on the bench and never got in the game."

As the election season began, Americans were much like Californians had been in 1966—unsure of their government, their economy, their traditions, and their nation's place in the world. The economy had endured a series of recessions for seven years that the government seemed powerless to stop. Inflation increased dramatically while unemployment went up. Factories across the Midwest closed down. Many middle-class Americans moved to the suburbs, while in the cities, poverty and crime increased. America's international role as a superpower also appeared to be in trouble. Nixon pulled the last troops out of Vietnam in 1973, and within two years Americans watched on TV as the North Vietnamese captured South Vietnam's capital. Ford had also continued Nixon's policy of détente, which meant negotiating with the Soviet Union to try to ratchet down the tension of the Cold War. But many Americans questioned the virtue of talks with their communist enemy.

With America doubting its leaders, Reagan had an excellent opportunity as an outsider with no Washington experience. But he quickly stumbled. After Reagan campaigned hard for more than a month in New Hampshire, Sears recommended he leave to stump in another state just two days before the primary. Reagan tended to trust his advisers, so he complied. He lost New Hampshire by just 1,317 votes out of 108,000. It was a narrow loss, but Ford had proved more resilient than expected. Within three weeks, thanks to his momentum, President Ford won primaries in four more states, including Florida and Reagan's birth state of Illinois. Under the direction of Ford's advisers, prominent Republicans began to tell reporters that Reagan should drop out so the party could unite behind Ford. At every campaign event, reporters asked Reagan when he was quitting.

While Reagan was cautious about getting into a race, now that he was in it his determination kicked in. "The question was should we quit," said Martin Anderson, Reagan's economic adviser. "And I think the general attitude was, it's not should we—it's do we have any choice. The consensus was you have to quit. And Reagan was just sitting there listening to this. 'I'm telling you right now,' [Reagan said] and he was looking at everybody in the room, 'that I am going to run in every single primary from here to the convention even if I lose every single one.' That is a point in time, in my mind, when you really saw the essence of Reagan's character."

Sears and pollster Richard Wirthlin had stayed up all night after the New Hampshire primary devising a new strategy. Reagan began criticizing Ford's foreign policy, arguing that détente with the Soviet Union was wrong, that communists could not be trusted. He passionately believed that the United States, despite losing in Vietnam, should not back away from being a world power. Speaking out on this made Reagan look more in control and like more of a leader. And it began to fire up conservatives.

But Reagan needed to win votes, and he needed

more money. No one wanted to donate to a losing cause, and Anderson estimated the campaign was $2 million in debt by mid-March. The next primary was in North Carolina at the end of the month. Many North Carolina Republicans were social conservatives, and liked that Reagan opposed abortion. Helped by his new fiery stump speech, Reagan won the primary with 52 percent of the vote. To raise money, he went on NBC a week later and gave his speech to a national audience, attacking Ford on the economy and on détente. It raised $1.5 million in donations. He went on to win the Texas primary, then Georgia, Alabama, and Indiana, followed by California.

It was too little too late, however. At the GOP convention in Kansas City, Ford received 1,187 delegate votes while Reagan received 1,070. He had narrowly lost. Ford invited Reagan down to the podium to speak, and to a wildly cheering crowd, Reagan urged the party to unite. The next day, as he and Nancy prepared to return to California, he spoke to his supporters. "The cause goes on," he said. "Nancy and I, we aren't going to go back and sit in our rocking chairs and say that's all for us."

Reagan still had work to do on the campaign trail

that fall. He had proven so popular with conservatives that several Republican congressional candidates asked him to come stump for them. Ford also asked Reagan for help on the campaign trail, though he and Reagan still had hard feelings toward each other. In November, Democrat Jimmy Carter narrowly beat Ford with 50.1 percent of the popular vote. Ford's pardon of Nixon probably made the difference, but the defeated president blamed Reagan for his loss.

Although Carter was taking the oath of office as America's thirty-ninth president, Reagan was in a better spot in January 1977 than a year earlier. He had lost the nomination fight but had impressed many Republicans outside California and was now being viewed as the presumptive nominee in 1980.

Some of his supporters immediately asked if they could start organizing for the 1980 election. He agreed, though he was not going to commit yet. "I wasn't the reluctant candidate I had been in 1965 and 1976—I wanted to be president," he later wrote. "But I really believed that what happened next wasn't up to me: If there was a real people's movement to get me to run, then I said I'd do it." In 1977, he formed a political action committee, a group that could raise money and communicate his ideas while he wasn't an official candidate, called Citizens for the Republic. Headed by Lyn Nofziger, the committee sent regular newsletters to supporters, keeping them up-to-date on Reagan's plans.

Reagan himself returned to working on his ranch, writing his column, giving his radio commentaries, and speaking. Mostly, he needed time to ride and think by himself.

Ron had started college at Yale, but when his parents visited him there at Thanksgiving, he announced he was dropping out to study ballet. Nancy had never heard him mention ballet before—he had always been a good writer, and she figured he would study that—but he insisted he had long wanted to be a dancer. Reagan was hurt by Ron's decision to drop out, but he and Nancy believed in letting their kids live their own lives, so they reached out to their friend Gene Kelly, one of Hollywood's most legendary dancers, to recommend a dance school for Ron in Los Angeles. He met a girl at the school—Doria Palmieri—who later followed him when he moved to New York and joined the Joffrey Ballet. He did have talent—Joffrey was a top group.

After years of rarely speaking to her family, Patti

moved back home for a few months and became closer to Nancy for a time. She also decided she wanted to follow in her parents' footsteps and become an actress. Nancy helped her join the Screen Actors Guild—she called herself Patricia Davis, using Nancy's maiden name, so she wouldn't be instantly identified as the Reagans' daughter. She eventually got a part in a theater production in Michigan but asked her parents not to come see it. They understood—if they came, all the attention would be on them.

On the other side of the country, President Carter was struggling, dogged by problems both at home and abroad. In January 1979, Iranian rebels overthrew Iran's monarch, the shah. The United States had long considered the shah an ally. Iran was rich in oil and located between the U.S.S.R.'s southern border and the Persian Gulf, where many other oil-rich nations sat, which made it a key Cold War friend. So even though the shah had used brutality to stay in power, the United States had given him military aid. When the shah was overthrown, a Shi'a Muslim cleric, the Ayatollah Ruhollah Khomeini, took power. The turbulence in Iran led to higher oil prices as supplies dwindled, and before long Americans were waiting in long lines at gas stations. Carter urged conservation, wearing a sweater while asking the nation to turn down their thermostats. The economy, already reeling from inflation and unemployment, worsened further.

The shah had gone into exile in Mexico, fleeing his country rather than face trial or execution, and was suffering from cancer. He asked Carter if he could seek medical treatment in New York. Carter agreed. Angered by Carter's asylum for the shah, a mob of young Iranians stormed the U.S. embassy in the capital of Tehran on November 4, 1979, taking sixty-six Americans inside hostage. They demanded that America send the shah to Tehran, return the great fortune he had supposedly taken with him, and apologize to the people of Iran. Khomeini ignored Carter's efforts to negotiate, and the crisis dragged on for over a year. The president—and America—looked helpless.

On another front, Carter had negotiated a nuclear-arms treaty with the Russians, which he thought was a positive step forward for détente. But in December 1979, the Soviets invaded Afghanistan in an effort to prop up a Communist regime. Carter was stunned.

While the United States had been trying to cultivate peaceful relations, the U.S.S.R. still appeared dedicated to world domination. Conservatives accused Carter of weakening America's security, and his approval rating sank to 32 percent.

Reagan declared his presidential candidacy, feeling confident. But even though he was the presumed favorite for the GOP nomination, he wasn't unchallenged. Nine other Republicans were running. Reagan's manager, John Sears, wanted Reagan to act the front-runner, so he had him campaign little for the first event, the Iowa caucuses. Another candidate, former Texas congressman and CIA director George H. W. Bush, blanketed Iowan Republicans with mail asking for their support. On caucus night, Bush won 33 percent of the vote while Reagan took just 30 percent.

Suddenly the press was asking whether Reagan really was the front-runner, and Bush gained momentum in the polls for the upcoming New Hampshire primary. Reporters also began asking if Reagan was too old to be president. Reagan had gotten a late start in politics, running for his first office at age fifty-five. But because he always looked young and athletic for his age, it had never been a concern. If he won in 1980, however, he would turn seventy a few weeks after he was inaugurated, making him the oldest president ever elected. The media wondered if his relaxed campaign schedule in Iowa was a sign he was too old to handle the rigors of the job.

Reagan realized his mistakes and changed his approach for New Hampshire. He was constantly on the campaign trail, and reporters complained they were exhausted from the pace, putting to rest questions of whether Reagan was too old. He loved campaigning and really was happiest speaking to the people, attacking Carter and promising to lead America to a brighter tomorrow. Reagan was energetic and focused when he participated in two Republican debates in New Hampshire. He answered questions well and looked like a man in charge, while Bush seemed ill prepared and aloof. On primary day, Reagan won 51 percent of the vote. Bush won just 22 percent.

After New Hampshire, Reagan's nomination was rarely in doubt. Bush was tougher than expected, but by the time Reagan won his boyhood state of Illinois in late March, his nomination was all but assured. He was able to spend the months before the convention reaching out to Republicans who hadn't supported him. He even met with Ford, who still blamed him for the 1976 loss. Reagan told Ford how hard he had once campaigned for him, then asked Ford to support him now. Ford agreed, and the two men, neither of whom could hold a grudge, became friends.

The Republican convention was marked by speculation over who Reagan would nominate for vice president. He needed a moderate running mate if he was going to appeal to less conservative voters. Many of Reagan's advisers suggested Bush, because he was moderate, came from electoral-vote-rich Texas, and had years of experience in Washington and foreign policy. Reagan had grown to dislike Bush during the primaries, but in the end he decided to ask him. Once they began working together on the campaign trail, Reagan changed his opinion of Bush—he was a loyal lieutenant, and his political knowledge was valuable.

After the convention, Reagan had a lead over Carter in most polls. The president continued to struggle—the hostages were still being held in Iran, and a rescue attempt in April had ended in disaster after a U.S. military helicopter collided with a support cargo plane in the Iranian desert, killing eight Americans. And the economy was in just as bad shape.

The Reagans rented a house in Virginia horse country as their home base on weekends—California was too far from most of their campaign stops. During the week, they were on the plane, with a full press corps, flying from state to state. As Reagan crisscrossed the country, he stressed two key points in his speeches. First, Carter had made America less safe overseas by not being tough enough with the Soviet Union and not keeping the military strong enough. Second, Carter had failed to fix the economy. Carter was proposing the same plans for big government that Democrats had been pushing for fifty years, while Reagan argued that the real solution to the recession was to cut taxes.

Reagan's proposals appealed to voters, but they still had questions about him. Was Reagan qualified? Could a former actor be president? With all his talk of being tough with the Soviets, would he lead America into a nuclear war? Was he too old? Reagan sometimes made misstatements on the campaign trail and got his facts mixed up, which added weight to these questions.

Carter knew he was unpopular, so his strategy was to

make voters think Reagan was worse. He accused Reagan of wanting tax cuts for the rich because he didn't care about the poor. But Reagan made voters feel better after a decade of doubting America, telling them that America's best days were still in front of it, that this was a special nation founded on the principle of freedom. It resonated with what many Americans believed.

On October 28, Reagan and Carter met for a TV debate. As always, Reagan looked at ease on TV. Carter looked nervous, spending his time accusing Reagan of being a conservative extremist. When he accused Reagan of campaigning in the 1960s against Medicare, the health-care plan for seniors, Reagan began his reply by saying, "There you go again." Reagan *had* campaigned for an alternative plan to Medicare, so he had been against the popular program. But what voters remembered was the quip and Reagan's charming, relaxed manner. He sounded more honest and more presidential than Carter. His response was graceful and effective. In his closing remarks, Reagan asked voters a simple question: "Are you better off now than you were four years ago?" Polls showed he won the debate by a two-to-one margin.

On the evening of election day, November 4, 1980, Nancy was in the bathtub and Reagan was in the shower in their California home, getting ready to go to dinner, when Nancy overheard a TV news report that the early results made it clear: Reagan had won. She jumped out of the tub and started banging on the shower door. The couple ran to watch the TV, wearing nothing but towels. Reagan had won the presidency with 50.7 percent of the popular vote and 489 electoral votes. He was going to Washington.

In the months before his inauguration, Reagan visited Washington three times, attending parties and meetings with members of Congress, lobbyists, bureaucrats, and members of the media, all people whose help he would need. He had learned from his time in Sacramento that he couldn't ignore legislators of either party if he wanted to get anything done. He met Tip O'Neill, the powerful speaker of the house and Democratic leader, who was friendly but warned him that he was now in the "big leagues"—things were not going to be as simple as in Sacramento. Reagan smiled politely, and he and O'Neill soon became friends.

Even though they fought politically, they always liked to trade stories and jokes.

Reagan wasn't bothered by O'Neill's comment, because he didn't mind being underestimated. Part of his charm was his ability to laugh at himself. He knew that people made fun of his age, his acting, and his relaxed work hours, so he turned the tables by making fun of himself. When a reporter asked him to autograph an old movie photo of him with Bonzo the chimp, he signed it and wrote, "I'm the one with the watch." He charmed a lot of potential adversaries during his Washington visits.

Reagan later told a reporter that throughout the ceremonies leading up to the inauguration, and then on the big day itself, he felt a strange "sense of unreality." Here it was, the biggest event in his life, and he didn't feel the excitement he thought he would. Nancy felt the same way. Maybe it was all too much to process. "Both of us kept thinking that there was going to come a moment when all of a sudden it hits us," Reagan said. "But things kept happening, and you still did not have that thing you thought would happen, that moment of awesomeness."

NINE

ON JANUARY 20, 1981, Carter and Reagan rode to the U.S. Capitol for the inauguration in one limo while Nancy and Rosalyn Carter rode in another. Carter didn't say a word—he was still bitter about losing and exhausted after spending the night negotiating to free the hostages, who were still in Iran. At the Capitol building, Bush was sworn in first. Reagan sat atop the western steps, looking out at the Mall, the Washington Monument, and the Lincoln Memorial, and marveling at the thousands of people gathered on an overcast day. He walked forward, and Nancy held up a tattered old Bible that his late mother had kept for decades. Nancy opened it to a passage that Nelle had underlined. Next to it Nelle had written, "A most wonderful verse for the healing of nations." Reagan put his hand on the Bible as

President Reagan is sworn in on the steps of the U.S. Capitol, Inauguration Day, January 20, 1981.

Supreme Court Chief Justice Warren Burger administered the oath of office; then as the crowd cheered and music played, he turned and kissed Nancy. He strode to the podium to give his inaugural address, and smiled as he looked at the sky. The sun had come out.

Reagan had always prided himself on writing his own speeches, but during the hectic rush of running for president, he had given in and let writers help. He still looked over each one and made heavy edits so that the words fit his political vision and his sense of cinematic style. Speechwriter Ken Khachigian had written the address, with extensive input from Reagan.

In it, Reagan called the nation to action, charging that the economy was in crisis and blaming excessive government intervention. "We must act today in order to preserve tomorrow," he said. "In this present crisis, government is not the solution to our problem. We are a nation that has a government—not the other way around." He pledged that he was not eliminating government, but restraining it so that individuals could freely work for a better economic tomorrow. "Let us renew our determination, our courage and our strength. And let us renew our faith and hope. We have every right to dream heroic dreams. . . . And as we renew ourselves here in our own land, we will be seen as having greater strength throughout the world. We will again be the exemplar of freedom and a beacon of hope."

At the end of his speech, the presidential party went into the Capitol to have lunch with members of Congress and guests. On the tables were small packs of jelly beans—the new president's favorite snack. During the lunch, Reagan announced that he had just learned that Carter's round-the-clock negotiations with Iran had freed the hostages after 444 days. A plane carrying them left Iran shortly after Reagan was sworn in.

He raised a glass to the former president, already on his way home to Georgia.

Reagan's party drove back to the White House and watched a parade, which included the high-school marching band from Dixon, Illinois, his alma mater. He felt tears in his eyes watching them. Then he and Nancy went up to the living quarters of the White House for the first time as its occupants. "I think it was only then, as Nancy and I walked hand in hand down the great Central Hall, that it hit home that I was president," Reagan later wrote. "It was only at this moment that I appreciated the enormity of what had happened to me. Maybe it was just recognizing our own furniture in the White House that did it. Maybe it had something to do with being reminded of my childhood by the Dixon High marching band. The depth of the emotion we felt at that moment is hard to describe. It packed a wallop. If I could do this, I thought, then truly any child in America had an opportunity to do it."

Within a few weeks, Reagan discovered he enjoyed being president. One of the first things he did was restore the pomp and circumstance of the job—flashy ceremonies and a band playing "Hail to the Chief" when he entered an event. These were trappings Carter and Ford had eliminated so that the president seemed less regal. But Reagan believed Americans wanted a regal leader.

He routinely wrote in his diary about his surprise over little perks of the job, like the staff on Air Force One always having clean clothes waiting for him if he sweated at an event, or pages having snacks ready during intermission at the ballet, when he went to see Ron perform. On a trip to New York City in March, he was amazed at the crowds of people waving to him from the sidewalks as he drove by. "I keep thinking that this can't continue and yet their warmth and affection seems so genuine that I get a lump in my throat. I pray constantly that I won't let them down."

Many good leaders have been overwhelmed with the responsibilities and pressure after becoming president. Not Reagan. He didn't let the job change him, though some of his staff wished he would improve his work habits. On the night before a major summit with several world leaders, Chief of Staff James Baker dropped off a big briefing book for Reagan. The next morning Baker returned and found the book untouched. When he complained, Reagan explained that the movie *The Sound of Music* had been on TV the night before. Reagan performed well at the summit despite the lack of studying.

Reagan firmly believed that his job was to focus on the big picture and delegate responsibilities. For the first six months of his presidency, Carter had personally reviewed every request to use the White House tennis court. Reagan knew how to use his time better. "He assembled people around him," said economic adviser Martin Anderson, "talked to them, made it clear to them what he wanted to do, and then the attitude seemed to be, OK, now you know what I want to do, let's do it. And he just assumed that these things would be done."

That attitude meant Reagan needed a good team. His chief of staff, Baker, organized everything—he decided what needed to be done in order to get Reagan's goals implemented, from overseeing the lobbying of Congress, to setting the agenda for cabinet meetings, to deciding when the president should hold a press conference or address the American public. Ed Meese, now a presidential counselor, was a sounding board for Baker and others because he had known Reagan for so long and knew what he wanted. Mike Deaver, the deputy chief of staff, was in charge of the president's schedule and planning public events. He had a knack for making these appearances very dramatic and effective—ensuring that TV coverage would make the president look like a heroic leading man.

Deaver was also Baker's liaison to Nancy, who continued to believe her responsibility was making sure the staff watched out for the president. She knew her husband only did well when he got eight hours of sleep a night and took breaks during the day. If the president was overscheduled and became irritable or tired, Nancy let Deaver know.

Meese, Baker, and Deaver—the troika, people dubbed them—wrote the script for Reagan's day. Every morning, he had a list of to-do items, and for meetings they came up with a rough script and printed the major points on four-by-six note cards, which Reagan referred to throughout. Some people he met with wondered why the president needed a script—anyone who knew Reagan knew that he was good at improvising and could think on his feet. But Reagan seemed happy to say his lines and stay on message.

Reagan's dependence on the troika had both good and bad points. On one hand, it kept him disciplined and focused. On the other, he never delved into details or tried to do his own research. He trusted the troika and his other staff implicitly. "Whenever somebody told him something, he assumed they were telling the truth," Anderson said. "I don't think he could conceive of people deliberately deceiving him or lying to him." Nancy knew this, too, which is why she was so protective.

Reagan quickly settled into a routine. He and Nancy woke up at seven thirty each morning, had breakfast, and read the *New York Times* and *Washington Post*. He'd take the elevator downstairs a few minutes before nine and walk on an outside path that led to his office. Sometimes he would stop and feed the squirrels. At nine, he met with Vice President Bush and his top aides to discuss the day. At nine thirty, his national security adviser briefed him on foreign affairs. The rest of his day was filled with meetings or phone calls with staff, his cabinet, foreign leaders, and members of Congress.

Lunch was a light meal at his desk, except on Thursdays, when he had lunch with Bush. Their relationship continued to strengthen—Bush believed in being a team player, in giving his advice to the president but supporting Reagan's policies even if they didn't match his own ideas. During the afternoon, Reagan would often take an hour off to answer mail from ordinary Americans. He loved to respond to requests from citizens, sometimes even writing personal checks if they asked him for financial help. His advisers found this both extraordinary and frightening. They didn't want people taking advantage of Reagan's kindness, but they quickly learned not to try and stop him. When Reagan discovered that a woman he had sent one hundred dollars to hadn't cashed the check because she wanted to save it as a memento, he told her to deposit it and made sure his accountant sent the canceled check back to her. Democrats found it equally incredible that Reagan, whose proposed budget would cut social programs for the poor, was all too happy to donate his own money—but the president's philosophy was that personal charity was better than government assistance.

Around five thirty, or "whenever work was done,"

Reagan would go upstairs, change clothes, and exercise in a bedroom they had converted into a gym. He'd shower, and unless there was a state banquet, he and Nancy ate their dinners on portable trays in front of the TV, watching the nightly news recorded by his staff. According to Nancy, they usually ate meat loaf, veal, steak, or lamb chops, and sometimes chicken or fish. "Ronnie" wouldn't eat liver, however, and he hated tomatoes. After dinner, he did more work in his study, going through paperwork or reading briefings. "After all our homework was done, we'd go to bed with a novel or another book, or I might pick up a magazine about horses, and we'd drop off to sleep about ten or eleven," he later wrote.

Reagan also liked to relax. On weekends he often went to Camp David, the president's retreat in Maryland, where he could ride horses. Even better were vacations to Rancho del Cielo. He still worked while there, but he could also change into his boots and jeans, ride (with a squad of Secret Service men on horseback nearby), chop brush, or work on the property. He spent 345 days of his eight years in office at Rancho del Cielo. Some in the media criticized all his vacation time, but Reagan felt the time outdoors reenergized him. His biggest complaint about the White House was that he couldn't be outside more.

Nancy also quickly settled into a routine in the White House. She had her own office and projects, including a program urging kids to "Just Say No" to drugs. The first thing she devoted herself to was renovating the White House itself. She had been shocked at how run-down the living quarters were when they moved in—nobody had renovated in decades. She began asking for private donations. Nancy and her decorator Ted Graber did most of the work, exploring federal storage facilities for historic pieces of furniture the government was not using. Work was done in the public spaces as well, and large portions of the mansion were rewired and fitted with modern air-conditioning. Visiting members of Congress, including O'Neill, began complimenting Nancy on how regal the president's house now looked.

Reagan's first focus was the economy, and his economic strategy had two parts. The first was his tax bill, which would cut income taxes by 30 percent for every taxpayer—10 percent a year for three years. It was a huge cut, but he firmly believed lower taxes would encourage Americans to spend their money on other things, stimulating the economy.

The second part was his budget. His tax cut would cost the government tens of billions of dollars each year, but Reagan had promised that he would enact a balanced budget. Government spending had to be reduced. Reagan wasn't worried—he had been arguing for years that the government was bloated and wasteful. There was one big budget exception, however. Reagan wanted to dramatically increase spending for the Department of Defense. In his opinion, the government had neglected the military since the Vietnam War. More importantly, he believed a large military buildup—including new nuclear weapons—was the only way to convince the Soviet Union's leaders that they could not win the Cold War.

Most Democrats did not like Reagan's economic plan. They saw the tax cuts as a giveaway to the rich and saw the spending cuts as a threat to programs that helped the needy—most of the cuts being discussed were to departments that aided the poor. All of that bothered Reagan, who couldn't stand being accused of being callous. He believed cutting taxes and shrinking government would create jobs, which would render those aid programs unnecessary. When the Democratic governor of New York told him in a meeting that his plan was going to make poor Americans suffer, Reagan lashed out, his face red. "I'm not going to sit still for the notion that we're hurting anyone. We've tried your way for decades and millions have been hurt by runaway inflation and unemployment."

To get Reagan's economic package enacted, Baker was in charge of lobbying Congress. He and his staff spent weeks calling and meeting with members of the House and Senate, asking what they needed to do to win their votes. Reagan's role was to persuade anyone who proved resistant. Calls from the leader of the free world had a way of swaying people's vote. Both bills were slowly working their way through committee—how quickly they came up for a vote, or if they came up for a vote at all, depended on Reagan's powers of persuasion. In the Senate, the Republicans had a majority, all of whom backed Reagan's plan. In the House, where the Democrats held control, it would be harder to find support.

☆ ☆ ☆

Early in the afternoon of March 30, 1981, Nancy was in the White House solarium when her lead Secret Service agent walked in. "There's been a shooting at the hotel," he said, referring to the Washington Hilton, where Reagan was giving a speech. "Some people were wounded, but your husband wasn't hit. Everybody's at the hospital." Nancy had already started moving toward the elevator, but the agent said she should probably stay there. "George," she said. "I'm going to that hospital. If you don't get me a car, I'm going to walk."

Reagan had been speaking to a labor union at the Hilton, and had exited the hotel just before 2:30 P.M., walking toward his limousine and waving to a small crowd of people. A man in the crowd began shooting—six shots in three seconds. The first hit Reagan press secretary James Brady in the head. The second hit a police officer in the back. The third flew over the president and hit a window across the street. The fourth hit a Secret Service agent in the abdomen. The fifth hit the limousine. The sixth ricocheted off the side of the limo and hit Reagan under his left arm. Those few seconds were a blur of noise and confusion as the Secret Service men ran to tackle the gunman and shield the president, pulling out pistols and machine guns. Before reporters could even begin to comprehend what had happened, Reagan's car was speeding away, with him and agent Jerry Parr inside.

When Parr realized Reagan was wounded, he directed the car to the hospital. Nancy arrived a short time later, and Deaver met her at the door. "He's been hit," he told her. "But they say it's not serious." Nancy wanted to see the president, but the doctors were still examining him and trying to stop the bleeding. "Mike," she said. "They don't know how it is with us. He has to know I'm here." But for the time being she had to wait. All she could think of was the day seventeen years earlier, when President Kennedy had been shot and killed in Dallas.

Eventually, after doctors had stabilized Reagan's breathing, she was led to his room. "Ronnie looked pale and gray," she later wrote. "Underneath the oxygen mask, his lips were caked with dried blood. He saw me, and pulled up the mask and whispered, 'Honey, I forgot to duck.' I was fighting tears too hard to smile, so I just leaned over and kissed him." Then she had to leave the room. They were taking him into surgery to try and remove the bullet. As he was wheeled past Baker and Deaver, he winked, and then asked, "Who's minding the store?"

Deaver had been with Reagan at the Hilton, while Baker was back at the White House. Deaver called Baker less than ten minutes after the shooting, and Baker immediately called several cabinet secretaries and told them to come to the White House to meet in the situation room, the special room underneath the White House used for national-security emergencies. No one knew if the shooting was a random attack or an orchestrated attempt to destabilize the country.

One of the first to arrive was Secretary of State Alexander Haig, a former Air Force general. Baker briefed him, then grabbed deputy press secretary Larry Speakes, Ed Meese, and Lyn Nofziger and headed to the hospital. Haig asked if the vice president had been called. Bush was in Texas and had heard from an assistant that the press was reporting a shooting, but that Reagan had not been hit. Haig got him on the phone and told him he should return to Washington. At 3:10 P.M., the White House issued a statement saying that the president had been shot but was stable. In fact, the situation looked grim for Reagan as he was taken into the operating room. The doctors told Speakes they believed Reagan was bleeding to death.

In the situation room, Haig, Defense Secretary Caspar Weinberger, Treasury Secretary Don Regan, and other top aides clustered around the table but were reduced to watching the TV for information. The media was having a hard time figuring out what was going on—three networks reported that Brady was dead, then retracted the report a few minutes later. A Secret Service agent pulled Don Regan aside and reported that the gunman they had taken into custody was a twenty-three-year-old named John Hinckley. The agents believed he was a loner, not part of an organized attack.

In the hospital, doctors had found and removed the flattened bullet from Reagan's chest, but he was still losing a lot of blood. They needed to operate again to stop the bleeding. Speakes returned to the White House at four P.M. and reporters surrounded him. He knew little of what was happening at the White House, and when they asked who was running the government, he replied, "I cannot answer that question at this time." Haig was watching on the TV downstairs and panicked, worried that the world would think the

U.S. government was incapacitated. He ran up the stairs, charged into the briefing room, and took over behind the podium. When a reporter asked who was in charge of the government while Reagan was on the operating table, Haig replied, "Constitutionally, gentlemen, you have the president, the vice president, and the secretary of state in that order, and should the president decide he wants to transfer the helm, he will do so. As of now, I am in control here, in the White House pending the arrival of the vice president and in close touch with him." Haig's answer was an honest attempt to reassure the nation, but his panting, wild-eyed performance made him look completely out of control. Moreover, the Constitution says that the speaker of the house and Senate president pro tempore both come before the secretary of state in succession.

An hour later, Nofziger stood in front of reporters at the hospital. The president was still in surgery, and he didn't have much new information, but he recounted what he did know of events earlier that afternoon, particularly Reagan's bravery and his one-liners to Nancy and the doctors. The reporters began chuckling—surely the president wasn't close to death if he was cracking jokes? Later Ron arrived at the hospital and went to his mother. He had been in Nebraska, sitting in a coffee shop, when he saw the news on TV and rushed to the airport with Doria. The rest of the kids were in California and were booked on morning flights.

Reagan woke up after seven P.M. in a great deal of pain, drugged, with a tube down his throat to help him breathe. All he could see was white—a white room, white sheets, people all dressed in white. For a split second, he wondered if he was in heaven. Then he vaguely remembered what had happened. Nancy and Ron came in to see him, and she broke down in tears. He was stable for now, however, and soon she went back to the White House. Outside the hospital were reporters and well-wishers. Some had hung signs on the building across the street that read WE LOVE YOU.

Bush landed at Andrews Air Force Base right as Reagan came out of surgery, and headed to the White House. Over the next few weeks, as Reagan recovered in the hospital, the administration continued to downplay how close to death he had been. They wanted the country to remain calm and not see Reagan as a weakened leader. Only after he returned to the White

House on April 11 did the real story begin to come out. Even then, the president's staffers exaggerated how much work he could do as he recovered.

All those who were shot survived, but Brady suffered a serious head wound. He was left paralyzed on one side of his body and confined to a wheelchair. Hinckley was later found not guilty by reason of insanity. He suffered from extreme depression and had attempted to kill Reagan to impress actress Jodie Foster, with whom he was obsessed. He was confined to a mental hospital, where he remains today.

Reagan wrote in his diary the night he came back to the White House, "Getting shot hurts. My fear was growing because no matter how hard I tried to breathe it seemed I was getting less and less air. I focused on that tiled ceiling and prayed. But I realized I couldn't ask for God's help while at the same time I felt hatred for the mixed up young man who shot me. We are all God's children and therefore equally beloved by him. I began to pray for his soul. . . . Whatever happens now, I owe my life to God and will try to serve him in every way I can."

Reagan's bravery and good humor while facing

death impressed the entire nation. Get-well cards and flowers poured in. *Washington Post* writer David Broder wrote, "A new legend has been born. The gunfire created a new hero in Reagan, the chipper 'Gipper' who took a .22-caliber slug in his chest but walked into the emergency room under his own power and joked with anxious doctors on his way into surgery. As long as people remember—and they will remember—no critic will be able to portray Reagan as a cruel or callow or heartless man."

Just nineteen days after being shot, Reagan was working from his bedroom. Soon he was calling Capitol Hill and pushing for his economic plan again. His approval rating was an overwhelming 75 percent, and he planned to use that popularity to keep Republicans in line and woo Democrats as his tax cut and budget bills moved through Congress. Less than a month after the assassination attempt, on April 28, Reagan stood in the House of Representatives for a special televised address to both houses of Congress. He was there to plug the tax cuts and budget plan, but Republicans and Democrats wanted to cheer for the heroic president. He joked later,

"That reception was almost worth getting shot for."

The assassination attempt did have long-term effects. Nancy was terrified someone else would try to kill Reagan. For weeks afterward, she broke down crying when he wasn't in the room. While she was talking about it with Merv Griffin, a TV producer and old Hollywood friend, he told her that an astrologer he knew had told him she had foreseen that March 30 would be a dangerous day for Reagan. Desperate for anything to help prevent another attack on her husband, Nancy called the astrologer, Joan Quigley, and began talking with her. Nancy had always read her horoscope, and while she wasn't sure she believed in astrology, she didn't think it could do any harm.

According to Nancy, at first she just spoke to Quigley like a patient to a therapist, sharing her concerns. Eventually, she began running her husband's travel schedule past the astrologer, who would tell her whether the dates were safe. Nancy would then ask Deaver to alter the schedule accordingly. After almost a year of this, Reagan walked into their bedroom one night as Nancy was finishing a call to Quigley. He asked her what the call was about and she explained. He said,

"If it makes you feel better, go ahead and do it. But be careful. It might look a little odd if it ever came out." If such an arrangement became public knowledge, the Reagans would be mocked—many Americans believe astrology is phony and silly—so only a few staffers knew. Deaver couldn't explain to others why he sometimes changed Reagan's schedule at the last moment.

The Secret Service became more worried about the president's safety as well. They began restricting his appearances and often made "Rawhide" (their code name for Reagan) wear a bulletproof vest, which he called his "iron underwear," if he was in public. Reagan stopped going to church on Sundays because it meant installing metal detectors and screening everyone attending the service. He didn't want to inconvenience his fellow worshippers.

Perhaps the biggest impact the shooting had was on Reagan's health. He had been in remarkable shape for a seventy-year-old man, and still was. But Ron and some friends noticed he was never the same after Hinckley's attack. He got tired more easily and needed naps. He couldn't concentrate as well.

☆ ☆ ☆

As Reagan's approval ratings soared, the momentum behind his economic package increased. Every time he made a speech to a crowd or on TV asking people to urge their representatives to support his plan, congressional phone switchboards would light up. In May, the House voted for his budget. The Senate then followed suit. A month later, both approved further spending cuts, for a combined total of $35 billion. Democratic House Majority Leader Jim Wright of Texas wrote about Reagan in his diary at the time, "What he preaches is pure economic pap, glossed over with uplifting homilies and inspirational chatter. I stand in awe nevertheless of his political skill. I am not sure I have seen its equal."

On July 16, the House approved Reagan's defense bill, raising the Pentagon's budget by $26.4 billion, the largest increase in history. Finally, on July 29, his tax cut plan—trimmed slightly to a 25 percent reduction over three years—passed. Reagan had fulfilled his biggest campaign promises, and voters, frustrated in the past decade by endless squabbling between the White House and Congress, were impressed by his ability to get things done.

Reagan believed the tax cuts and budget would be the biggest accomplishment of his presidency because it would fundamentally reshape citizens' relationship with the government. Individuals would have more freedom and the government would shrink. But Reagan didn't realize he had a big problem: his budget numbers did not add up.

Reagan had hired a young congressman named Dave Stockman to head the Office of Management and Budget (OMB), and Stockman's job was to find enough budget cuts to pay for the tax reductions and defense spending increases. The yearly federal budget at that time was $700 billion. As *Atlantic* magazine writer William Greider explained in an article on Stockman, forty-eight cents of each of those dollars were used for benefit checks—Social Security, pensions for retired soldiers and government workers, aid for the disabled. Reagan had promised voters he wouldn't touch any of those popular programs, and Congress was unlikely to approve cuts to them. About twenty-five cents paid for national defense, and Reagan had increased that to almost thirty cents. And ten cents went to paying interest on the national debt. "That left seventeen cents for everything else that Washington does," wrote Greider. "The FBI and the national parks, the county agents and the Foreign Service and the Weather Bureau— all the traditional operations of government—consumed only nine cents of the dollar. The remaining eight cents provided all of the grants to state and local governments, [from] aiding handicapped children [to] building highways." Those programs cost a total of $120 billion, and Stockman had to find $40 billion to cut, and almost every one of those programs had someone—a cabinet member, a congressman, or a senator—who thought it was invaluable.

When Reagan, Stockman, and the rest of the cabinet had met throughout the spring to discuss the budget, the president signed off eagerly on Stockman's proposed cuts. But at later meetings, the cabinet secretaries complained about the cuts and tried to explain to Reagan why their programs were necessary. Attorney General William French Smith fought an OMB proposal to cut two thousand of the Justice Department's 54,000 employees by saying, "The Justice Department is not a domestic agency. It is the internal arm of the nation's defense." Reagan responded, "Bill is right. Law enforcement is something that we have always believed is a legitimate function of government." He rejected the cut. But everyone thought what their own agency did was a legitimate function of government. Many of the tough reductions never got made, particularly to popular aid programs for businesses and subsidies for farmers. The programs that were cut or shrunk were mostly aid for the poor, including subsidized school lunches, job training for the unemployed, food stamps, and housing assistance.

When the tax cuts passed that summer, Stockman told Reagan and the cabinet that the deficit for 1982 was growing larger than expected, rapidly approaching $100 billion. He suggested Reagan give up on his balanced budget pledge. Reagan said no. Stockman introduced possible trims to defense spending. Reagan said no. Stockman said $20 billion a year could be raised in new small taxes on items like tobacco and alcohol. Reagan said no new taxes. Meese began talking about how when Reagan was governor they had balanced the budget by cutting government staff. Stockman tried to explain that unlike in California, staff salaries were a small percentage of the federal budget and cuts to them wouldn't solve the deficit, but Reagan didn't listen. "The federal government is lathered in fat when it comes to employment," he said. He told the cabinet to explore staff reductions, but the directive went nowhere.

When Reagan had begun his first term as governor, he had said that solutions to government problems are simple, just not easy. That was not true when it came to the federal budget, and Reagan's lack of experience and knowledge showed in his attempts to trim it. He simply did not comprehend how complex the budget was. He thought it was filled with wasteful programs that could easily be terminated—but the programs he thought wasteful were just a tiny percentage of the budget, and each one had a defender in Congress. If Reagan really wanted to shrink the budget, he would have had to tackle one of the bigger expenditures—Social Security or national defense. But he was unwilling to do so. During Reagan's time in office, government expenditures increased at a slower rate than during Carter's administration, but they still increased. And the tax cuts meant a lot less money to pay for those expenditures.

When Stockman tried to teach all this to Reagan, the president tuned out or fell back on the same rote answers—cut staff, eliminate waste. He would sometimes doodle during meetings or let his attention wander. Reagan could be very intelligent on certain topics—especially if the facts were presented to him in a narrative or anecdotal fashion. But arcane budget issues bored him.

The disagreements between Stockman and other cabinet members also revealed a flaw in Reagan's corporate management style. Reagan liked to say he would let his cabinet members argue about something, listen to all sides, and then decide based on their arguments. But when both sides had good points, Reagan found it hard to choose. His aides would argue passionately, the president would say he had to think about it, and nothing would be resolved.

That fall, as the economy stagnated and the deficit swelled, the stock market tumbled as investors lost faith in Reagan's economic policies. The recession worsened. Unemployment rose to almost 10.8 percent. Early in 1982, the media began reporting on the growing number of homeless and other poor Americans struggling with the recession and less federal aid thanks to Reagan's budget cuts of programs like food stamps and housing assistance. The president's approval rating was going downhill. While Reagan's policies probably did little to cause the recession, his deficit spending sapped investors' confidence, and his budget cuts reduced aid to the poor just when more people needed it.

Reagan was hurt by the criticism, but he blamed the media, not his policies. He believed the economy was going through a hangover thanks to excessive government in the 1970s, and that his job was to keep a positive attitude, just as FDR had done during the Depression. He also showed a lack of sensitivity when it came to those most hurt by the recession, at one point saying that many homeless people chose to be homeless. Reagan, who had managed to find a job during the Great Depression after only a few months, had a difficult time understanding that some people tried hard but still couldn't find work.

When the media and Democrats also went after Nancy and her renovations of the White House, Reagan got angry. Nancy had raised a million dollars in private donations to improve the living quarters, restoring antique furniture and replacing the china used for state dinners. The money was almost all private, but many felt it unseemly for the First Lady to buy china and carpeting while people were homeless. Nancy was hurt by these reports—she believed the media was creating a false image of her: "That I was a rich, fancy woman who kept acquiring more and more expensive items," she later wrote. She withdrew for a while, speaking rarely to reporters. It took a few years before she realized the best way to disprove the image was to open up to the media. "I wish the press had taken a little more time to get to know me better. And I also wish I had tried harder to communicate to them who I really was."

No matter how much the media, Democrats, Republicans, and even his own staff began to question his policies, Reagan continued to believe his plan would work in the end. In January 1982, he wrote in his diary that he could tell the new year would be a tough one—Republican congressional leaders had met with him and asked him to raise taxes. Everyone in Washington believed it was the only way to fix things—everyone except Reagan. He continued to refuse.

It took until August 1982, when the Republican-controlled Senate rejected his budget and instead proposed a $99 billion tax increase on cigarettes, phone calls, medical expenses, and businesses, for Reagan to realize he had no choice. He could either look like he had lost control of the country as Congress passed a budget and tax increases, or he could back the plan he believed was the least damaging. When Reagan signed the bill on August 19, he felt defeated. Americans thought his economic policies had failed and he was signaling a partial retreat.

The stock market improved after the bill passed, but the economy was still hurting. In November, Republicans lost twenty-five seats in the House, a big loss that was blamed on the president. Political analysts were saying that Reagan would never be reelected in 1984—that Republicans should start looking for another candidate. By January of 1983, Reagan's pollster informed him that his approval rating was at its lowest point ever—35 percent. Reagan patted him on the arm and said, "I know what I can do about that. I'll go out and get shot again."

TEN

THOUGH REAGAN DEVOTED most of his energy to the economy during his first two years in office, no president can avoid dealing with foreign affairs. By 1981, the Cold War between the United States and the Soviet Union had raged for more than thirty years. The two superpowers had enough nuclear weapons to obliterate the planet several times over. But because a nuclear war would probably destroy most life on Earth, the United States and U.S.S.R. never got into a direct war. It was a principle called Mutual Assured Destruction, or M.A.D., and it was what kept the Cold War cold.

Reagan had never believed in détente—he wanted to win the Cold War. The biggest difference between Reagan and his predecessors was that most had accepted that communism was here to stay. Communists had ruled Russia since 1917, Eastern Europe had been communist since the end of World War II, and China since 1949. But ever since his days in Hollywood, Reagan had felt that communism was a corrupt, impractical system that would eventually fail.

Reagan's plan was to strengthen the U.S. military and build more nuclear weapons. By 1985, the defense budget was double what it had been in 1980—the Pentagon was spending $34 million an hour. Reagan knew the Soviets would start building new weapons to try and match the United States, but he believed that since capitalism was stronger than communism, the Soviets would damage their economy trying to keep up. Only then did he think they would negotiate in good faith for arms reductions. Reagan believed he was building more bombs so that eventually there would be fewer bombs.

In his speeches, Reagan made it clear that he did not accept communism as a legitimate form of government. Nor did he believe the Cold War was permanent. In May 1981, at Notre Dame University, he said, "The West won't contain communism, it will transcend communism. It won't bother to denounce it, it will dismiss it as some bizarre chapter in human history whose last pages are even now being written." In an address to the British Parliament in June 1982, Reagan said, "It is the Soviet Union that runs against the tide of human history by denying human freedom and human dignity to its citizens." Reagan predicted that the Russian economy would crumble and that the people of Eastern Europe would rise up against the Soviets and overthrow their rule.

But the speech was widely ignored as yet another example of Reagan's "cowboy talk," as his critics called it. They argued that Reagan's speeches and defense buildup were worsening relations between the superpowers and heightening the risk of a nuclear war. Polls showed that one of Americans' biggest concerns about Reagan was that he would start a war with the U.S.S.R. A movement to stop his nuclear-weapons buildup started.

Reagan's hostility toward communism wasn't limited to the Russians. In 1979, a Nicaraguan communist group called the Sandinistas overthrew the country's dictatorial leader, Anastasio Somoza. Conservatives worried that the Sandinista government was a Soviet and Cuban puppet. On January 10, 1981, communist fighters in neighboring El Salvador launched a military campaign to try and topple that country's pro-American government. The Sandinistas were aiding them. Reagan believed the fighting in El Salvador was proof that the Sandinistas, with backing from Cuba and the U.S.S.R., were trying to spread communism throughout Central America. "El Salvador and Nicaragua were only a down payment," Reagan later wrote. "Honduras, Guatemala and Costa Rica were next, and then would come Mexico."

Reagan didn't want to get directly involved because he knew that Americans would have little tolerance for sending troops to fight communists in a third world jungle—it was too reminiscent of Vietnam. Instead, he sent military advisers and financial aid to El Salvador, and turned to the CIA. In December 1981, he secretly authorized Agency director Bill Casey to give $19 million to the Contras, a rebel group in Nicaragua that opposed the Sandinistas. The money would pay for training for them in Honduras, where they could also launch attacks on the Sandinistas. Reagan ignored the fact that many Contra leaders had belonged to the brutal Somoza regime—he believed the Sandinistas were far worse. The Contras "are the moral equal of our founding fathers and the brave men and women of the French resistance," he later wrote. "We cannot turn away from them." It was the first of many covert attempts to help the Contras.

Aside from communism, Reagan was not particularly knowledgeable about foreign affairs when he became president. When Judge Bill Clark, who had been Reagan's chief of staff in California, became national security adviser late in 1981, he realized the president still had little idea of what was going on overseas. But Clark knew how to frame ideas in a way that appealed to Reagan—so he took the president to the movies. Clark borrowed instructional films from the State and Defense departments on topics like the Soviet Union and the Middle East conflict. He then asked CIA director Bill Casey to have his analysts put together films on various world leaders. "It was far more interesting to see a movie on [Indian leader Indira] Gandhi covering her life than sitting down with the usual tome the Agency would produce," Clark later said. "And that would spark questions from the president that I could fire back to the Agency."

Some advisers mocked Clark's methods, but others took them to heart. Before several of Reagan's summits, various advisers would pretend to be world leaders with whom Reagan would be meeting, and act out an "improv" with the president. George Shultz, who replaced Al Haig as secretary of state in 1982, would brief Reagan before meetings with other leaders by telling him what his motivation in the "scene" was.

Reagan's critics charged that these tactics showed he was an actor, just reciting lines. But the truth was more complex than that. Most politicians in Washington had been lawyers or academics before serving in government. They approached issues from an abstract, analytical point of view. To Reagan, personal stories were far more illuminating than endless intellectual debate. Reagan didn't think there was anything wrong with what his advisers were doing, and he ignored any critics who questioned his intelligence. He knew what his strengths were and thought they made up for any weaknesses he had.

☆ ☆ ☆

Unfortunately Reagan's strengths did not help him when he was suddenly faced with a crisis in the Middle East. Israel was America's closest ally in the region, and when it got involved in the civil war of its northern neighbor, Lebanon, Reagan's administration was unwittingly dragged in as well.

For many years, the Palestine Liberation Organization (PLO), a terrorist group/militia that wanted to replace Israel with a Palestinian state, had controlled large parts of southern Lebanon and launched regular attacks on Israel from just across the border. Lebanon's government had no control over the PLO, because since 1975 the country had been torn apart by a civil war between various Christian, Sunni Muslim, Shi'a Muslim, and Druze factions. The government of Syria, another enemy of Israel, had invaded and occupied parts of Lebanon in 1976, and the chaos gave the PLO more freedom to strike Israel.

In the summer of 1981, PLO fighters made several attacks, and the Israeli Air Force responded by launching a series of bombing strikes on the Lebanese capital, Beirut. Some of the bombs, which were directed at

PLO headquarters, ended up killing hundreds of civilians. After learning of the bombings, Reagan watched reports showing the dead and wounded on TV, and decided that Israel was responding too forcefully. He asked his special diplomatic envoy to the region, Philip Habib, to ask the Israeli government to stop. The Israelis agreed, and a cease-fire took effect a week later.

Reagan had always been a strong supporter of Israel. "The Holocaust, I believe, left America with a moral responsibility to ensure that what happened to the Jews under Hitler never happens again," he later wrote. But in the fall of 1981, the PLO and Israel kept exchanging attacks, and civilians kept dying. Reagan had come into office pushing for peace in the Middle East because he believed instability in the oil-rich region benefited the Soviets. But his hopes for peace were fading. For the rest of 1981 and the first five months of 1982, Habib worked to negotiate a more permanent cease-fire between Lebanon, Israel, and Syria, with little luck. Reagan began to hear reports from his intelligence experts that the Israeli prime minister, Menachem Begin, was planning to invade Lebanon to attack the PLO. Reagan urged Begin to show restraint.

"Israel's response," Reagan later wrote, "was, in effect: Mind your own business."

On June 6, 1982, Reagan was in Europe when he learned that Israel had invaded Lebanon. Israeli military leaders told the media that they only intended to occupy the southern portion of the country, creating a buffer zone from PLO attacks. But their tanks kept moving north. Reagan was so busy meeting with European leaders that he barely had time to hear from his advisers what was going on. Meanwhile, Israeli troops closed in on Beirut. Countries around the world protested Israel's actions as the media showed people in Beirut suffering as their city was encircled. Reagan asked Begin to stop the advance, but Israeli forces completely surrounded Beirut, trapping PLO leaders inside. "Boy, that guy makes it hard to be his friend," Reagan said of Begin.

Israel began bombing West Beirut, and cut off food and electricity. U.S. public opinion slowly turned against Israel. One day the Israelis bombed and shelled parts of the city for eleven straight hours. Reagan was sickened by the footage of the carnage and asked an assistant to get Begin on the phone. "Menachem, this is a holocaust," Reagan said. Begin replied, "Mr. President, I think I know what a holocaust is." In a furious voice—which most aides had never heard—Reagan told Begin that Israel was being inhumane and destroying its image in the world. Begin hung up, only to call back twenty minutes later—he had ordered the bombing stopped. Reagan said to an aide, "I didn't know I had that kind of power."

Reagan wanted to find a way to make this new cease-fire last. Secretary of State Shultz and other advisers told him that the best way was to send U.S. Marines to Beirut as part of a peacekeeping mission to enforce the cease-fire among all factions. Defense Secretary Weinberger opposed the idea from the start—Lebanon was a complicated situation to insert U.S. soldiers into. But Reagan couldn't watch the bloodshed anymore and not intervene. After discussing the idea with the leaders of Italy and France and most of the fighting factions in Lebanon, he announced that a multinational peacekeeping force (MNF) made up of American, French, and Italian soldiers would go to Beirut to maintain peace. In addition, the PLO's leadership made an agreement with international negotiators to leave Lebanon.

Reagan hoped a stable cease-fire would allow time for negotiations to broker an end to the civil war and a Syrian and Israeli withdrawal.

The MNF arrived at the end of August. PLO leaders and many of its fighters left for Tunisia, and Lebanon's parliament elected a new president, Bashir Gemayel, a Christian militia leader. Gemayel was an ally of Israel and the United States who Reagan hoped could help to end the civil war. Reagan and Shultz began developing a larger Middle East peace plan, and with the cease-fire holding, on September 10 the MNF left Beirut for their transport ships. Weinberger wanted the Marines out as soon as possible. "As the summer of 1982 came to an end," Reagan later wrote, "I still felt cautiously optimistic about the future of the Middle East."

But establishing a lasting peace was more difficult than Reagan thought. On September 14, a bomb exploded in East Beirut, destroying a building and killing Gemayel. The next day Israel reentered West Beirut, violating the cease-fire. Meanwhile, Gemayel's militia moved into a Palestinian refugee camp in the city and murdered more than seven hundred people, many of them women and children—the militia believed PLO fighters who had been hiding in the camps were responsible for the assassination of Gemayel. The Israelis, who were stationed outside the camps, stood by and let it happen.

Reagan watched the events on TV, like the rest of the world, in horror. He ordered the MNF back in, hoping it could reestablish the cease-fire. Reagan wanted to give the Lebanese government, now led by Gemayel's brother Amin Gemayel, enough time and security to gain control of its nation. The MNF's "purpose is not to act as a police force, but to make it possible for the lawful authorities of Lebanon to discharge those duties," he said. He also wanted to convince both the Israelis and the Syrians to withdraw.

Reagan's decision showed a lack of understanding of the complex realities of Lebanon. Many Lebanese did not see their Christian president as a lawful authority. Gemayel didn't act like one either—he used his office and American support to turn the Lebanese Army into a division of his own militia. And Syria had no intention of leaving Lebanon. When the MNF, including the U.S. Marines, began backing the Lebanese government army, it became an enemy of the other militias and the Syrians. The marines now had targets on their backs, and on April 18, 1983, a delivery van packed with dynamite exploded outside the U.S. embassy in Beirut. The middle of the building collapsed, killing sixty-three people, including seventeen Americans. U.S. intelligence agents suspected the bombing was the work of a Shi'a militia group—Hezbollah—which had the backing of both Syria and Iran.

Reagan went to Andrews Air Force Base outside Washington when the American victims' bodies arrived five days later. He and Nancy met the family members. "We were both in tears. All I could do was grip their hands. I was too choked up to speak," he later wrote. That night he was supposed to go to the White House correspondents dinner, an annual evening of joking with the press corps. He put on his tux and attended but asked their pardon for not making jokes. For once, Reagan had no funny stories.

But Reagan did not want to let terrorists scare him out of Lebanon. As 1983 wore on, the marines became more aggressive in helping the government army fight the other factions, which responded by firing random

The Reagans walk past coffins of victims of the Beirut U.S. embassy bombing during a memorial service at Andrews Air Force Base.

shells at marine bases, or taking sniper shots at solitary marines on the street. Each time a marine died, Reagan called his parents to console them. One father asked him, "Are we in Lebanon for any reason worth my son's life?" Reagan said yes. "America is a country whose people have always believed we had a special responsibility to try and bring peace and democracy to others in the world. That's what our marines are doing in the Middle East."

Reagan once described October 23, 1983, as the saddest day of his life. He was asleep at 2:27 A.M. when the phone rang. Several hours earlier, a smiling young man driving a yellow truck had sped past the guard post outside a marine barracks in Beirut and into the lobby. The truck exploded with awesome power, and the entire building, with 350 marines sleeping inside, collapsed. The bodies of 241 dead marines were found in the rubble. Terrorists had struck again.

Reagan knew how to fight the Cold War, but like most Americans, he was confused and angered by Islamist terrorism. He didn't know how to retaliate against a shadowy organization like Hezbollah. Public opinion was turning against the military's involvement in Lebanon quickly, and it was almost 1984—election year. Reagan's advisers told him there was no clear solution in Lebanon and that the marines were doing little good. On February 7, 1984, Reagan ordered the troops to withdraw to their ships. America's involvement in Lebanon was effectively finished.

The bombing of the marine barracks was the most devastating tragedy of Reagan's presidency, and it troubled him deeply. For a few days afterward, his staff was concerned about how distraught he looked. At one meeting with aides he tried to read a letter from the father of a marine who had been killed, but he was too upset to continue.

The American public was upset, too, but was quickly distracted by another U.S. military action, this one closer to home. Just days after the Lebanon bombing, Reagan sent U.S. troops to the tiny Caribbean island chain nation of Grenada. The country was in the middle of a violent Communist-led rebellion, and Reagan worried that the Soviets and Cubans would use Grenada to spread communism throughout the Caribbean. And eight hundred Americans were trapped on the main island. U.S. troops easily defeated the Communists and rescued the Americans. Reagan and the military had acted quickly and decisively, and his approval ratings went up.

Reagan was enjoying an even bigger victory at home in the fall of 1983—for six months the economy had been improving. In fact, the end of the recession was the start of a boom that would last almost uninterrupted until 1990. Reagan felt vindicated for never losing faith in his economic plan. His popularity soared, even though he had still not managed to balance the budget.

The defense buildup had continued even in the rough economic times, and new nuclear missiles had been deployed in Europe. Critics still accused Reagan of being a loose cannon who might start a nuclear war, but Reagan continued to believe his nuclear buildup was actually a path to peace.

Reagan had another idea for preventing a nuclear war—for years, he had been suggesting that American scientists should try to develop a defense against nuclear weapons—a way to shoot down missiles before they hit their targets. Even if America was stronger than the Soviets, why live under the risk of nuclear war? What if some mad dictator got his hands on nuclear weapons and decided to attack the United States? During a meeting in February 1983, the Joint Chiefs of Staff told Reagan that they supported using Pentagon dollars to research a possible missile-defense shield, a system of lasers or other missiles that could take out ballistic nuclear missiles. They warned him that any potential system was years away, but Reagan loved the idea and wanted to announce it to the public immediately. On March 23, 1983, in a nationally televised speech, Reagan introduced the research program, which was known as the Strategic Defense Initiative (SDI).

The public was completely surprised—few people had ever heard of such a concept. The press, after interviewing scientists who said such a system was years if not decades away, made fun of Reagan's space shield, dubbing it "Star Wars." None of Reagan's advisers thought SDI was realistic, either. But they saw it as a potential bargaining chip—in negotiations with the Soviets, they could offer to abandon SDI research in return for concessions. Reagan did not see it as a bargaining chip, however—he really believed that such a system was possible, and that the United States had to develop it to ensure the world would never be destroyed by nuclear war. Though he didn't tell his advisers, he dreamed that he might share the technology with the Soviets, guaranteeing peace between the two powers and enabling them to abandon nuclear weapons for good. That was Reagan's real goal—the end of the threat of nuclear war.

Soviet leaders had a different reaction to Reagan's SDI announcement. They had been beaten technologically by the United States before: when the United

States developed the first atomic bomb, and when it had landed on the moon. They feared that if Reagan was able to deploy a defense system, the United States could launch a nuclear attack on the Soviets with no fear of retaliation because the SDI shield would protect them. Shortly after Reagan's speech, a Soviet intelligence alert was issued—all Soviet agents should look for signs of an impending attack. The Soviet military was so worried that when a South Korean airliner drifted into Soviet airspace accidentally, the military shot it down, killing 269 people.

Reagan didn't blindly hate the Russians, but his efforts to reach out to Soviet leaders had gone nowhere. One problem was the unstable leadership of the U.S.S.R. Leonid Brezhnev, the Soviet premier when Reagan took office, had ruled since 1964 and was old and ill. He suffered a stroke in March 1982 and died eight months later. His successor, Yuri Andropov, died fifteen months after taking power. Konstantin Chernenko ruled for thirteen months. Reagan finally joked that he wanted to negotiate with the Soviets but they kept dying.

Before the presidential campaign started in 1984, Nancy tried to convince her husband not to run again. "I yearned for more family time and more privacy," she later wrote. "I missed my friends and family, and I missed California." But Reagan felt differently—there was a lot more he hoped to accomplish. After several nights of discussing it, Nancy could see that he really wanted to do it, so she told him he had her support.

The president was well positioned for reelection. Most Americans approved of his performance, the economy was booming, but just as importantly, after the uncertainties of the 1970s, Reagan had made the country proud of itself again. He campaigned on that, with a series of commercials that began with the line "It's morning in America" and showed idyllic scenes of people going to work, or raising the flag. Reagan did not propose many new ideas for his second term, but it didn't seem to matter.

After a long primary battle, the Democrats nominated Walter Mondale for president. A former senator from Minnesota, Mondale had served as Jimmy Carter's vice president. He was an ethical, well-regarded politician, but his campaign did not know how to counter

Reagan's optimistic message. Mondale said he would raise taxes to close the deficit, an unpopular idea. He accused Reagan of being dangerous in his tough talk against the Soviets. He nominated the first female vice presidential candidate from a major party, Geraldine Ferraro, which was well received but did not move his poll numbers significantly higher.

Reagan did show one moment of vulnerability, however. On October 7, in the first of two presidential debates, he looked confused. He was tired and wasn't as prepared as he should have been. People started speculating that at seventy-three, Reagan might be too old for a second term. Nancy was furious. She blamed the staff for overworking him during debate rehearsals. "Ronnie has always been an inspiring leader who outlines broad themes," she later wrote. "But his staff had spent weeks cramming him full of statistics. 'What have you done to my husband?' I said to Mike Deaver angrily."

Reagan learned his lesson. He prepared for the second debate but focused on his overall themes. And his advisers worked hard to make him feel relaxed and confident. On October 21, at the second debate, when age came up, Reagan quickly pounced. "I will not make age an issue of this campaign. I am not going to exploit, for political purposes, my opponent's youth and inexperience." Even Mondale laughed, though he knew he was beaten.

On November 6, 1984, Reagan won one of the biggest landslides in U.S. history with 58.8 percent of the popular vote, and every state except Mondale's home state of Minnesota and the District of Columbia. Millions of lifelong Democrats voted for Reagan—to them, his leadership qualities were more important than partisan politics. The American people wanted to give the Gipper one more term.

President Reagan and Soviet General Secretary Gorbachev in Red Square during the Moscow Summit, May 31, 1988.

ELEVEN

"A PRESIDENT IN his second term, even after a landslide, has a much briefer honeymoon and a less effective mandate than after his first election," wrote former president Richard Nixon in a private memo to Reagan shortly before his 1985 inauguration. Nixon knew this lesson well. Two years after being reelected in a landslide, he had resigned to avoid impeachment.

Reagan had achieved many of his objectives in his first term, but after four years, many top members of his staff were worn out. Mike Deaver, James Baker, and several other advisers felt that while Reagan was a friendly boss, he never made any effort to truly get close to his staff and rarely recognized their hard work. Most suspected that if they walked out of the Oval Office and never returned, Reagan would not notice.

Baker, who may have been the most capable White House chief of staff in history, needed a change of scenery and wanted to work outside the White House in a top cabinet position. He and Treasury Secretary Don Regan decided to switch jobs—they proposed the idea to Reagan, who approved it. Deaver left his job four months into the second term. He had worked for the Reagans for decades, but the stress had gotten to him—unknown to anyone, he was suffering from alcoholism. Meese soon left to become attorney general. Reagan accepted all these changes with little reflection. He had always been very dependent on his staff, yet he did not consider that their departure might affect his performance. He was the star of the show, and a few cast changes seemed no big deal to him.

In late January, Reagan sat down for lunch with Regan and reviewed the major goals he wanted to accomplish in his second term. Reagan wanted to cut the budget and reduce the deficit, reform the tax code, resist communism in Central America, try to improve the situation in the Middle East, and negotiate a nuclear arms reduction treaty with the Soviets. It was an ambitious list that would require a shrewd chief of staff. At the lunch, Regan gave his boss a proposal for streamlining White House operations. "I approved the plan," Reagan wrote later, "not realizing how much it would enlarge Regan's powers at the expense of others on the staff, restrict access to me, and lead to problems later on."

Regan had been a very effective manager both as a Wall Street executive and then as Treasury secretary. He wanted to control who saw the president, and did not court the press or other politicians as Baker had done. "Don Regan was a tyrant," White House political adviser Ed Rollins later said. "He thought of himself as deputy president."

Nancy quickly began hearing complaints. "They told me [Regan] had poor relations with Congress and the media," she later wrote. "That he was restricting their access to the President. That he was explosive and difficult to deal with. That he was intimidating his subordinates. And that good, experienced people were starting to leave the West Wing because they couldn't work with him." She told these people to talk to her husband, but Regan let no one meet with the president alone. She mentioned the complaints to her husband, but he never took them seriously. The president was so dependent on his chief of staff that he never actively tried to find out if these rumors were true.

Regan's first test at helping the president navigate a crisis came early in the second term. In May, Reagan was scheduled to travel to West Germany to meet with chancellor Helmut Kohl and other world leaders for a summit. While there, he and Kohl would mark the fortieth anniversary of the Nazis' surrender to Allied forces, which ended World War II in Europe. As the trip was being planned, Kohl proposed to Reagan that they commemorate the anniversary and celebrate American–West German friendship by laying a wreath at a military cemetery.

Reporters soon discovered that the cemetery, Bitburg, was the final resting place of not just drafted German soldiers, but also members of the SS, Hitler's elite units, some of whom were suspected war criminals. Jewish-American groups began complaining about the visit. Reagan ignored the criticism—he felt he was trying to show that the war was over. More importantly, he had promised Kohl he would go, and Reagan hated to break a promise.

The media kept reporting on the issue, Democrats in Congress passed a resolution condemning the visit, and even Republican senators were calling the White House and urging Regan to tell the president to reconsider, but the chief of staff ignored the requests. Eventually, Reagan agreed to add a visit to a concentration camp to his schedule to show he was not insensitive to the Nazis' victims. Despite this solution, criticism of the Bitburg visit continued long after the trip, damaging Reagan's popularity.

On March 10, 1985, Soviet leader Konstantin Chernenko died, and Mikhail Gorbachev succeeded him. Reagan sent Secretary of State Shultz and Vice President Bush to Chernenko's funeral, carrying a letter for Gorbachev. In it, Reagan wrote that he wanted to work with Gorbachev on nuclear-arms reductions. He also invited Gorbachev to Washington for a meeting. Gorbachev wrote back in just two weeks, saying that while he was not ready for a summit yet, he did believe the two should work together and meet in person soon. Reagan quickly wrote back. For the next four years, the men would write to each other frequently.

Gorbachev was fifty-four, the youngest Soviet leader in five decades. He had been born to a family of peasants in southern Russia during Joseph Stalin's reign. (Both of his grandfathers were imprisoned for a time by Stalin's government.) He was very intelligent, and with his engaging personality he quickly became a rising star in the Communist Party.

The Soviet leaders who selected Gorbachev as premier hoped this young leader could reenergize the nation, and Gorbachev quickly impressed many people. The British prime minister, Margaret Thatcher, Reagan's closest foreign ally, told the American president that Gorbachev was someone Reagan could "do business with." In April, Reagan again invited Gorbachev to meet for a summit. Gorbachev agreed, and the two leaders planned to meet in November in Geneva, Switzerland. Reagan believed that if he could meet a Soviet leader in person, and connect with him on a human level, he could finally begin to make progress in nuclear-arms reductions.

During the summer of 1985, Reagan was more focused on the Middle East than on the Soviet Union. He had withdrawn American soldiers from Lebanon in 1984, hoping to end U.S. entanglement in the civil war. But on June 14, 1985, TWA flight 847 was flying from Athens to Rome when two Lebanese men hijacked the plane with 153 passengers and crew on board, most of them Americans. For three days, the plane flew back and forth between Beirut and Algiers, a city in North Africa. Most of the passengers were gradually released, but when the hijackers realized that one American passenger was a U.S. Navy diver, they beat him, shot him in the head, and dumped his body on the runway.

On June 16, the plane landed in Beirut again. Most hostages were released, but thirty-nine were held for two weeks in Beirut by a Shi'a militia leader while Reagan and his staff tried to negotiate their freedom. Reagan was deeply frustrated by his powerlessness. He had no hope of rescuing the hostages by force, so he had to talk to other nations' leaders and hope they could secure their release. The militia leader demanded that the Israelis free more than seven hundred Shi'a prisoners in return for the hostages. Israel was prepared to do so, but Reagan had pledged that he would not make concessions to terrorists. He was also afraid, however, that if he didn't secure their release somehow, the American people would lose faith in him. Finally, on June 30, a deal was struck between the militia leader, Syria, Israel, and the United States. The hostages were sent to Syria, which released them. Meanwhile, the Israelis quietly released their prisoners over the next few weeks, claiming the action was unrelated.

While Reagan was relieved about the deal, he was still upset. "Americans were still captive in Lebanon, and I was determined to get them home," he later wrote. Since the beginning of 1984, seven Americans had been taken hostage in Beirut by various shadowy groups. Years later, all evidence suggests that most of the groups were fronts for Hezbollah. "I learned how helpless the head of the most powerful nation on earth can feel," Reagan later wrote. "No problem was more frustrating for me when I was President." Reagan met with the family of one of the hostages that summer, and they angrily accused him of not doing enough. The president was upset for days afterward.

On July 3, National Security Adviser Robert "Bud" McFarlane met with an Israeli official who had a surprising idea. The official told him that an exiled

Iranian named Manucher Ghorbanifar claimed to be in contact with moderate members of the Iranian government who wanted to improve relations with the United States. According to Ghorbanifar, they were worried that when the current Iranian leader, Ayatollah Ruhollah Khomeini, died, Iran would fall into chaos. They proposed to secure the release of one or more of the American hostages in Lebanon, and in return, the United States would sell them weapons— Iran was in the middle of an eight-year war with Iraq.

The Reagan administration had a firm policy that Iran's government was a sponsor of terrorism and should not be dealt with. But McFarlane had long hoped for better relations with Iran because it sat between the Soviet Union and the Persian Gulf, the region where most of the world's precious oil came from. Most U.S. intelligence agencies, however, did not believe there were any "moderates" in the Iranian government. And Ghorbanifar had approached the CIA with supposed information about hostages before. He failed several polygraph tests and was labeled a "fabricator" by the Agency. But McFarlane was interested in the idea and started plans to present it to the president.

☆ ☆ ☆

A week after McFarlane's meeting, Reagan was worrying about other matters. He was in the hospital for a minor procedure—doctors had spotted a small polyp in his colon during a regular checkup and were removing it. After the procedure, Reagan was making jokes when the doctors came into his room. The White House physician asked Nancy to come outside to speak with him. He explained that while they were removing the polyp, they had noticed a much larger one farther up his colon. It looked like it might be cancerous, and if they didn't remove it, cancer could quickly spread. Removing it would be far more intrusive, involving surgery. Nancy and the doctor went back in and explained the situation to the patient. The doctor suggested they perform the surgery first thing the next morning. Reagan smiled and said, "Does this mean I won't be getting dinner tonight?"

Early the next day, Reagan signed papers transferring presidential authority to George Bush for eight hours. Then the doctors gave him anesthesia and started the surgery. After a few hours, it was over—they had removed the polyp and two feet of Reagan's lower intestine, leaving a long scar on his stomach. A biopsy showed the polyp was cancerous, but the doctors believed he would be fine. In his usual optimistic view of things, Reagan denied he had cancer when reporters asked him about it—he had had something cancerous in him, but now it was gone. He stayed in the hospital for a week but still worked. On July 17, he wrote in his diary, "Some strange soundings are coming from some Iranians. Bud M. will be here tomorrow to talk about it. It could be a breakthrough on getting our seven kidnap victims back."

McFarlane presented the idea of working with the moderate Iranians to other advisers and the president in Reagan's hospital room the next day. The advisers were split on whether it was prudent to try to improve relations with Iran. Several questioned whether the United States would be selling arms to the very people sponsoring Hezbollah's kidnappings. But Reagan seized on the idea that a deal could help release the captives. "He wanted to get the hostages out," Shultz said later. "And his staff people who worked on him, I believe, did exactly what staff people shouldn't do. They knew he had a soft spot for the hostages." Reagan told MacFarlane to pursue the idea.

Everything was set up covertly—if the media found

out that the administration was dealing with Iran, it would have been considered a scandal. On August 20, 1985, Israel sent ninety-six American-made antitank missiles to Iran, and the United States supplied new missiles to Israel to replace the ones sold to Iran. (Using the Israelis as middlemen made sense. No one would question an arms sale to Israel.) Iran paid Israel for the missiles, and Israel paid the United States for its new missiles. No hostages were released, however. Reagan was on a three-week vacation on his ranch, with most of his family, when McFarlane called on August 24. "I received a 'secret' phone call from Bud McFarlane," Reagan wrote in his diaries. "It seems a man high up in the Iranian govt. believes he can deliver all or part of the 7 kidnap victims in Lebanon sometime in early Sept. I had some decisions to make about a few points—but they were easy to make. Now we wait."

On September 14, a second shipment, of 408 missiles, was sent, and the next day, Reverend Benjamin Weir was released near the U.S. embassy in Beirut. The remaining hostages were supposed to be freed soon afterward but were not. The Iranians then asked for more weapons. Reagan, happy about Weir's release, authorized McFarlane to continue.

☆ ☆ ☆

Reagan spent much of his time that fall preparing for his November summit in Geneva with Gorbachev. He saw it as one of the most important performances of his career, and for once, he did his homework. For six months beforehand, McFarlane gave Reagan briefing papers covering all aspects of Soviet society, from the economy to their military to their psychology. Reagan read them eagerly and also consulted with Nixon, who had negotiated with the Soviets several times and always took a practical approach.

Reagan arrived in Geneva on November 16, 1985, three days early so he could recover from any jet lag—ever since he had fallen asleep while meeting with the pope in 1982, his staff made sure he had extra time to adjust to time changes. He was excited. "Lord I hope I'm ready," he wrote in his diary. Conservatives back in Washington were scared—they believed any arms treaty with the Soviets was a trap. Gorbachev arrived in Geneva worried about his country. The Soviet Union was in trouble—its economy was weak from fighting a war in Afghanistan and competing with the United States in an arms race. The Soviet people were standing in long lines outside grocery stores, waiting for the little food there was. For decades, Reagan had said communism would not work, and he was being proven right. For Gorbachev, slowing down the arms race would give his country economic breathing room. He could spend less on weapons and more on his people's basic needs.

Around ten A.M. on November 19, Gorbachev arrived at the nineteenth-century lakeside chateau lent to the leaders for the summit. Reagan walked outside to greet him. "As we shook hands for the first time, I had to admit," Reagan later wrote, "that there was something likable about Gorbachev. There was warmth in his face and his style, not the coldness bordering on hatred I'd seen in most senior Soviet officials I'd met."

To begin the summit, the two men were scheduled to meet with just their interpreters present for fifteen minutes. Instead, they chatted for over an hour. Gorbachev stressed that the two nations had to learn to coexist and to make sure nuclear war was never fought. Reagan agreed and said the main purpose of their summit should be to eliminate suspicions toward each other. Then they moved to a larger conference room to join their advisers.

For two days, the leaders discussed the issues that divided their countries and how to ratchet down the tension of the Cold War. Reagan criticized human rights in the Soviet Union—urging Gorbachev to allow more freedom. Gorbachev replied that this was none of Reagan's business, and that homeless people in America didn't seem to have equal human rights. On weapons, both Reagan and Gorbachev expressed a desire to reduce the number of nuclear weapons their militaries had. But there was a big roadblock in the way—SDI, or "Star Wars." Gorbachev insisted that no agreement could be made as long as the Americans pursued such a defense system. To the Soviets, it was not a defense but a weapon, because with the shield in place, America could attack the Soviets, or threaten to, with little fear of reprisal. Gorbachev also knew his country did not have the money to try and keep up with the United States on SDI research. He hoped to kill it now.

Here Reagan's stubbornness kicked in. He wanted SDI so that the American people could always feel safe from nuclear holocaust. He was idealistic about this and even promised Gorbachev that America would share the SDI technology with the Soviets so both nations could be safe. Gorbachev dismissed this—how was he supposed to believe America would share such an advantage? Reagan had really meant what he said and was hurt by Gorbachev's response. (His advisers did not tell him, but they agreed with Gorbachev—there was little chance the American people would approve of sharing such technology with an enemy.)

On the morning of the third day, Reagan and Gorbachev issued a joint statement that they would continue to work together to improve U.S.-Soviet relations, but no agreement was reached. Any deal would have to wait for future summits.

Something important *had* been achieved, however—Reagan and Gorbachev learned they liked each other. On the afternoon of the first day, Reagan invited Gorbachev to come to Washington for a future summit. Gorbachev agreed and invited Reagan to Moscow. Neither side had expected two future summits to be agreed to. While the two men still had strong differences, they had begun to trust each other.

Early in 1986, the Reagans received an advance copy of a novel Patti had written called *Home Front*.

It was fiction but was about a liberal woman whose conservative father was California governor and then president. The woman's mother was difficult, obsessed with appearances. Nancy was upset—she and Patti had grown closer two years earlier, when Patti had married her yoga instructor. The book was a complete surprise. "I read it with sorrow and anger," Nancy later wrote. "It was a thinly disguised, self-pitying autobiographical novel." Reagan never revealed his thoughts on the book to anyone. When reporters asked him about it, he just replied that it was fiction.

When Patti went on a media tour for the book, Nancy grew more furious. Patti called Ron to ask why she had not heard from their parents, and he responded, "You've trashed us all in a terrible book. You made Mom and Dad into cartoon characters. Did you expect them to call you and tell you it's great!" He hung up, and neither he nor Nancy spoke to Patti for several years. Ron had stopped dancing a few years earlier and begun a career in journalism, writing stories for magazines and reporting on *Good Morning America*. When he was next on the show, he was asked about Patti, and said, "I think Patti's book was wrong and in bad taste."

☆ ☆ ☆

In the months after the Geneva summit, Reagan's and Gorbachev's negotiators continued to try and move arms talks forward, but they made little headway. In September, Gorbachev suggested they have a summit in England or Iceland to try and break their impasse. Once they had an agreement, they could have a summit in Washington. Reagan agreed.

On October 9, Reagan arrived in Reykjavik, Iceland, eager to meet with Gorbachev again. Gorbachev came prepared. In the first meeting, he suggested they agree to cut nuclear weapons by 50 percent, and remove all intermediate-range nuclear missiles from Europe. In return, SDI research would be confined to laboratories—no tests—for ten years. "He's brought a lot of proposals, but I'm afraid he's going after SDI," Reagan told Shultz.

As Reagan's and Gorbachev's advisers met and tried to hash out details of an agreement during the next two days, it became clear the Soviets were willing to make significant concessions. For Gorbachev it all came down to SDI, and Reagan would not yield—it was his insurance policy if the Soviets did not honor an agreement and destroy their missiles.

"I realized he had brought me to Iceland with one purpose: to kill the Strategic Defense Initiative," Reagan later wrote. "'The meeting is over,' I said." Reagan stood up and put on his coat. "Can't we do something about this?" Gorbachev said. "It's too late," responded Reagan. The summit was over.

In the November 1986 elections, Democrats gained a majority in the Senate. Reagan would have to deal with a Democratic-controlled Congress for his final two years in office. But an event two days before the elections proved even more important. Just after midnight, on November 2, 1986, Reagan was sleeping at his ranch in California when the phone woke him. It was John Poindexter, a retired Navy admiral who had replaced McFarlane as national security adviser. Poindexter told Reagan that an American hostage, David Jacobsen, had been released after seventeen months of captivity in Beirut.

For fifteen months, McFarlane, Poindexter, and their deputy Oliver North had been secretly negotiating with Ghorbanifar and the so-called Iranian moderates for the release of the hostages and improved American-Iranian relations. At several stages they had sought approval from Reagan to proceed, which he granted. In May, McFarlane (no longer NSA, but still working on the project) and North flew to Tehran in a top secret operation and met with Iranian government officials. During this visit, McFarlane realized they were not dealing with Iranian moderates but members of Iran's Revolutionary Guard—Islamist men who were totally loyal to the Ayatollah. Other advisers became aware of this, too, but North and Poindexter continued the negotiations.

All of this effort, which completely violated the Reagan administration's embargo on dealing with Iran, produced little. The United States sold Iran a total of 2,004 antitank missiles, and spare parts for antiaircraft missiles for $30 million, while only three hostages were released. And during the same period, three more Americans had been kidnapped in Beirut.

The day after Jacobsen's release, a Lebanese magazine reported about McFarlane's mission to Tehran, claiming that was the reason for the release. By the morning of November 5, the story was in newspapers all over the world. When reporters asked Reagan whether he had made a deal with Iran, the president replied, "No comment" and then told them that their speculation on the story might be damaging U.S. efforts to free other hostages. The media kept digging into the story.

Reagan believed the media accounts were false and endangering the hostages. The press was reporting that the president was selling weapons to the radical supporters of the Ayatollah, the very people who had taken Americans captive. But Reagan believed that he was dealing with moderates in the Iranian government who could influence the terrorists. Based on McFarlane's and North's encounters, however, it appeared the Americans had been duped by the Iranians.

McFarlane's original idea may have been to improve relations with Iran, but Reagan had always been more interested in the potential to free the hostages. Now that the press was calling it a scandal, Reagan insisted that it was an effort to improve relations. He was in denial, falling back on a version of the truth that he found more comforting because he didn't want to face facts. "This whole irresponsible press bilge about hostages and Iran has gotten totally out of hand," he wrote in his diary. "The media looks like it's trying to create another Watergate."

Chief of Staff Don Regan decided that Reagan should go on TV and address the people—this had always been the president's best weapon. But he failed to realize that the president was in denial and believed a version of events that didn't match the facts. To make matters worse, no one in the White House—not Regan, not the president—knew all the details of the Iran negotiations. McFarlane, Poindexter, and North had been operating secretly and independently. When the president's speechwriter asked North and Poindexter for the full facts of the Iran operation, they provided a completely inaccurate story—they thought the best strategy was to cover up the whole affair. The president was given a speech full of lies, and any reporter following the story would know. Reagan delivered his speech from the Oval Office on November 13. He again called the media reports false and dangerous and explained the weapons sales as an attempt to reach out to Iranian moderates. "We did not—repeat, did not—trade weapons or anything else for hostages," he said.

Polls afterward showed that more than 70 percent of the public did not believe him. Most thought Reagan had negotiated with terrorists. His pollster told him that he could have sold weapons to the Soviets and done less damage. Reagan's diary entries show he continued to believe the press was inventing the whole scandal.

As attorney general, Ed Meese was the nation's top law-enforcement official. It was his responsibility to decide if any laws had been broken in the negotiations with Iran. Meese quickly announced he would start an investigation but moved slowly and later admitted he was more interested in making sure the president was not in legal trouble than in going after lawbreakers. North spent several days shredding papers and destroying evidence before Meese's assistants showed up in his office. But they did find a damaging document that didn't get shredded. It showed that the United States had been overcharging the Iranians—they paid $30 million for weapons worth only $12 million. North had diverted almost $4 million to the Contras, the Nicaraguan rebel force. The rest of the money had disappeared into Swiss bank accounts, much of it going to pay various middlemen.

Reagan had been fighting with Congress since his

first term for funds to support the Contras. He had appealed to the American people several times—warning them that he believed the Communist government of Nicaragua was a threat. When Congress denied funds, he had appealed to others for help. Allied governments, such as Saudi Arabia, and private individuals made donations to the Contra cause. CIA operatives were covertly helping the group. By diverting federal money to the Contras, though, North had broken the law. And if Reagan had approved such a move, he had broken the law, too, and could be impeached.

Reagan did not remember ever approving North's diversion of funds, and investigations never found proof that he did. But North's shredding of documents destroyed much of the evidence. Reagan wrote in his diary on November 24, "North didn't tell me about this. Worst of all John Poindexter found out about it & didn't tell me." The next day, Poindexter resigned and Reagan fired North. The president and his staff knew they had to go public with what North had done—and promise an independent investigation—or Congress would be calling for an impeachment trial. Reagan appointed a bipartisan commission headed by former Senator John Tower to investigate what was now called the Iran-Contra Affair.

But Reagan still blamed the media for the scandal, telling *Time* magazine, "This whole thing boils down to a great irresponsibility on the part of the press." Reagan's usual response to a crisis was to stubbornly defend his own actions. But his refusal to face facts and admit that the Iran negotiations were wrong prevented the administration from moving on to other issues— every day was consumed by media and congressional questions about Iran-Contra. The day before Thanksgiving, at an event where he pardoned a live turkey, reporters barraged him with Iran-Contra questions. "I felt I was the one being roasted," he said afterward. His approval rating quickly fell from 70 percent to 46 percent. His honesty, which American voters had always called his most valuable asset, was damaged. "He never had his integrity questioned before," Nancy later said. "And that really, really bothered him."

The Iran-Contra Affair—both the weapons sales to Iran and the funding of the Contras—was investigated by the Tower Board, an independent counsel, and a congressional committee. When the Tower

Board questioned Reagan, they were shocked at his poor recollection of events, but there was no evidence showing he had approved the money transfer to the Contras.

Nancy was still worried about her husband's low approval ratings, however. As long as the country questioned her husband's honesty, he could not move on to other goals. She blamed Don Regan. The chief of staff's management style—his short temper, his arrogance, and his efforts to keep other staff members away from the president—had sheltered Reagan from advice that might have prevented this scandal. Regan had tried to be in control of everyone on staff, including the National Security Council, but in reality he had not been in control. Worse, once the scandal broke, Regan's strategy was to ignore it, repeat the same denials to all questions, and try to change the subject. He refused to understand that Reagan needed to admit to the country that he had made a mistake. Nancy wanted her husband to fire Regan, but he hated firing people when times got rough. Even Ron urged his father to clean house. But Reagan resisted.

On February 25, the Tower Board members presented their findings to the president, giving him a last chance to comment before they were released to the public. They showed that the details of the operation left no doubt that it was a swap of weapons for hostages. And they said that Regan's failed efforts to assert tight control over the White House staff had led to the chaos that allowed the scandal to happen. Reagan finally suggested to his chief of staff that he resign. Regan grew angry, complaining that Reagan was throwing him to the wolves, but he agreed to step down in a week.

Just a few days later, though, word leaked to the media that Reagan had already asked former Senate majority leader Howard Baker to be his next chief of staff, and Regan immediately resigned. He and Reagan never spoke again, and in 1988, he published a book giving his version of events. The book also revealed Nancy's reliance on astrologer Joan Quigley for scheduling advice. For months, reporters asked whether astrology was influencing the president's decision making.

Baker quickly proved to be a good chief of staff and a calming presence. While packing up their offices, Regan's aides told him that Reagan was old and senile and no longer capable of holding office, but when Baker and his staff sat down and engaged the president, they immediately found him energetic, bright, and firmly in charge. On March 4, Reagan went on TV to address the American people again. "A few months ago I told the American people I did not trade arms for hostages. My heart and my best intentions still tell me that's true, but the facts and the evidence tell me it is not. . . . There are reasons why it happened, but no excuses. It was a mistake." One poll showed Reagan's approval rating jumped nine points after his speech. He had started to repair his connection to the American people. But Iran-Contra did have long-term effects on Reagan's presidency. With his approval ratings damaged, Democrats in Congress were able to more effectively oppose his policies.

Reagan later wrote, "I still believe that the policy that led us to attempt to open up a channel to moderate Iranians wasn't wrong. Nevertheless, mistakes were made in the implementation of this policy. Because I was so concerned with getting the hostages home, I may not have asked enough questions about how the Iranian initiative was being conducted. I trusted our people to obey the law."

He never fully accepted that what he had done was

wrong—in fact, he always insisted after that March 4 speech that there was no swap of weapons for hostages. He had created his own version of what had happened in his mind, like the imagined baseball game he had created years ago on the radio where the batter fouls off one pitch after another. "Reagan is a classic model of the successful child of an alcoholic," biographer Lou Cannon later said. "He doesn't hear things and doesn't see things that he doesn't want to see and hear."

In October 1987, Reagan was confronted with another personal crisis. During a routine mammogram, doctors found a tumor in Nancy's left breast. She scheduled surgery for twelve days later, telling the doctors that if it was cancerous, she wanted a mastectomy—her breast would be removed completely. She also asked the White House physician to tell her husband. He later said that when he told Reagan, the president's face held an expression he'd never forget. Reagan had never considered that he might lose Nancy.

On October 17, while Reagan and Nancy's brother waited outside, doctors operated on her. The tumor was malignant, so they removed her left breast. The operation was a success. When she woke up afterward, she saw her husband and said, "My breast is gone," worried that he would see her as less of a woman. "It doesn't matter," he replied, kissing her forehead, "I love *you*." Her recovery took several months, but the cancer was gone.

Since Reagan had first met Gorbachev, he had wanted to make a breakthrough agreement on nuclear-arms reductions. Months of stalled negotiations had left him frustrated, but on February 28, 1987, Gorbachev made a concession on SDI. He announced that while he would not agree to an overall arms reduction without limits on SDI, he would agree to a treaty eliminating all intermediate-range nuclear missiles in Europe. Details had to be ironed out, but the first treaty reducing the number of nuclear weapons was possible.

Just because they were making progress on arms talks didn't mean Reagan was going to stop calling for changes in the Soviet Union, though, especially with respect to human rights. In every meeting with Gorbachev, Reagan asked him to improve human rights in the U.S.S.R. and Eastern Europe—to release dissidents from jail and to allow people who wished to emigrate to other countries the freedom to do so.

In June, Reagan embarked on a ten-day tour of Europe, and toward the end, he visited West Berlin and the Berlin Wall—the border between Western and Eastern Europe. Almost all the Eastern European governments were still puppet states that took orders from the Soviets. In a speech he gave in front of the Berlin Wall, Reagan admitted that Gorbachev was slowly allowing more freedom in the Soviet Union but asked if it was just a show. Reagan called on Gorbachev to give freedom to the peoples of Eastern Europe and the U.S.S.R. "General Secretary Gorbachev, if you seek peace, if you seek prosperity for the Soviet Union and Eastern Europe, if you seek liberalization: Come here to this gate! Mr. Gorbachev, open this gate! Mr. Gorbachev, tear down this wall!"

His words were heard around the world. Gorbachev was trying to increase freedom—but he was also trying to keep the communist system in power. Reagan's speech made it clear that the free world would accept nothing less than real liberty.

On December 7, Gorbachev arrived in Washington, D.C., for a three-day summit. By now the two leaders were friendly, trading jokes as they signed the Intermediate-Range Nuclear Forces Treaty (INF). They had several meetings afterward, trying to make progress on a 50 percent reduction of all weapons, but SDI was still a problem. Gorbachev seemed to accept that Reagan would never compromise on that. They had gone as far as they could, and in thirteen months, Reagan's successor would be in the Oval Office. But the treaty was a remarkable accomplishment. Some conservatives decried it because they preferred the security of the Cold War and worried that Gorbachev's reforms were all a deception. But most Americans wanted better U.S.-Soviet relations, and they trusted Reagan to represent them. After all, if Ronald Reagan could trust the leader of the Soviet Union, maybe an end to the Cold War was possible.

While Gorbachev was in Washington, he was treated like a rock star by the American people. Reagan received similar treatment in May 1988, when he and Nancy flew to Moscow for one final summit with Gorbachev. Reagan spoke out forcefully on human rights. He met with people who had been punished for speaking out against communism and "refuseniks"—those who wanted to emigrate but had been denied the right. Wherever he went, Muscovites lined the streets to see him.

At Moscow State University, he spoke to students. "Freedom is the right to question and change the established way of doing things. It is the right to put forth an idea, scoffed at by the experts, and watch it catch fire among the people. It is the right to dream—to follow your dream and conscience, even if you're only one in a sea of doubters. Your generation is living in one of the most exciting, hopeful times in Soviet history. It is a time when the first breath of freedom stirs the air and the heart beats to the accelerated rhythm of hope. . . . We may be allowed to hope that the marvelous sound of a new openness will keep rising, ringing through, leading to a new world of reconciliation, friendship and peace."

As Reagan finished his second presidential term, he could look back on many accomplishments and several failures. Eight years earlier, he had asked Americans to "dream heroic dreams again," and they had. Most people were confident about the future of the country, and believed its role in the world was to spread freedom. Reagan's speech at Moscow University—the heart of the Soviet Union—may as well have been called the Reagan Doctrine.

TWELVE

AT 9:50 A.M. on January 20, 1989, Ronald Wilson Reagan walked into the Oval Office for one last look around. He left a note in the desk drawer for his successor. George H. W. Bush, Reagan's vice president, had been elected president. Reagan considered it one more victory.

After the inauguration ceremonies, he and Nancy boarded a helicopter on the White House lawn. It took off and swooped over the White House. Reagan turned to Nancy, who was crying, and said, "There's our little bungalow down there."

They flew to Andrews Air Force Base and from there to Los Angeles. "Then home & the start of a new life," Reagan wrote in his diary that night.

He was happy to be retired. He worked on his autobiography, rode his horses, and worked on the ranch.

He also kept watching as the world changed. That fall, democracy movements sprang up all over Eastern Europe. Gorbachev refused to intervene with troops as past Soviet leaders had done. The Communist governments in Eastern Europe fell, and Germans tore down the Berlin Wall themselves. Germany reunified in 1990. In 1991, hard-line Communist politicians and military leaders tried to overthrow Gorbachev and end his reforms, but the Russian people resisted and the coup failed. Gorbachev's hold on power was weakened, and in just a few months, the Soviet Union dissolved into fifteen nations, including Russia, Ukraine, and Kazakhstan. The Cold War was over.

In 1993 Reagan began to suffer from memory problems. He started to repeat himself and to speak as if he were in episodes of his past for short periods. In November 1994 he issued a letter to the nation saying that he was suffering from Alzheimer's disease. The disease was little known at that time. Many people thought it was a form of senility, but it is actually a disease that attacks the brain. The cause is still unknown.

In his letter, Reagan wrote, "At the moment I feel just fine. I intend to live the remainder of the years God gives me on this earth doing the things that I

Ronald and Nancy sitting by Lake Lucky at Rancho del Cielo, on a dock he built himself.

have always done. I will continue to share my life's journey with Nancy and my family. . . . I only wish there was some way I could spare Nancy from this painful experience. . . .

"In closing let me thank you, the American people, for giving me the great honor of allowing me to serve you as your President. When the Lord calls me home, whenever that may be, I will leave with the greatest love for this country of ours and eternal optimism for its future. I now begin the journey that will lead me into the sunset of my life. I know that for America there will always be a bright dawn ahead."

Nancy continued to care for Reagan as his mental condition deteriorated, with the help of a nurse. His children still visited, even Patti, who reconciled with her parents in 1993. Maureen saw him often, until she passed away from cancer in 2001. Reagan was a strong man, and he lived for almost ten years. But his memories were gone. All his stories and anecdotes were gone. He could no longer recognize his own children.

On June 5, 2004, Reagan died of pneumonia. After a state funeral in Washington and an outpouring of grief, his body was buried on the grounds of the Ronald Reagan Presidential Library in Simi Valley, California.

His burial site is inscribed with a quote from him, one his mother Nelle would have been proud of. "I know in my heart that man is good. That what is right will always eventually triumph. And there's purpose and worth to each and every life."

SOURCE NOTES

INTRODUCTION

"What the hell's . . .": Reeves, *President Reagan*, 34.

"Jerry, get off . . ." and "You not only . . .": Reagan, *An American Life*, 259–60.

"I can't breathe": Reeves, *President Reagan*, 35.

"Honey, I forgot . . .": Reagan, *An American Life*, 260.

"Don't worry about . . .": Broder, "Reagan Wounded by Assailant's Bullet."

"I hope you're . . ." and "Mr. President, we're . . .": Reagan, *An American Life*, 261.

CHAPTER ONE

"I came home . . ." "She said Jack . . ." and "For a moment . . .": Reagan, *An American Life*, 33.

"As I look . . .": Reagan, *An American Life*, 29.

"He looks like . . ." and "No one I . . .": Reagan, *An American Life*, 21.

"She always expected . . .": Reagan, *An American Life*, 22.

"for the cat": Cannon, *Governor Reagan*, 12.

"I was a little introverted . . .": Reagan, *An American Life*, 31.

"I found a . . .": Skinner, *Reagan: A Life in Letters*, 6.

"I don't remember . . .": Reagan, *An American Life*, 35.

"The next instant . . .": Reagan, *An American Life*, 36.

"Life is just . . .": Cannon, *Governor Reagan*, 21.

CHAPTER TWO

"Although my grades . . .": Reagan, *An American Life*, 53.

"had a personality . . .": Cannon, *Governor Reagan*, 31.

"Those were cheerless . . .": Reagan, *An American Life*, 19.

"How in the hell . . .": Cannon, *Governor Reagan*, 35.

"Could ye tell . . ." and "Here we are . . .": Reagan, *An American Life*, 64–65.

"The only thing . . .": McPherson, *To the Best of My Ability*, 416.

"During his fireside . . .": Reagan, *An American Life*, 66.

"Margaret's decision shattered . . .": Reagan, *An American Life*, 76.

"It might contain . . ." "If the Cubs . . ." and "I saw Curly . . .": Wills, *Reagan's America*, 109.

"Take off your glasses": Reagan, *An American Life*, 79.

"Sign before they . . .": Reagan, *An American Life*, 81.

CHAPTER THREE

"How about Ronald?": Reagan, *An American Life*, 83.

"I was there . . .": Reagan, *An American Life*, 94.

CHAPTER FOUR

"Yes, and you'd . . .": Reagan, *An American Life*, 97.

"Now I knew . . .": Reagan, *An American Life*, 115.

"Many fine people . . .": Reagan, *An American Life*, 114–15.

"We're through. We're . . ." "Nothing—and everything . . ." and
    "Perhaps I should . . .": Cannon, *Governor Reagan*, 72.

"Finally, there was . . .": Cannon, *Governor Reagan*, 73.

CHAPTER FIVE

"despondent, in a . . .": Cannon, *Governor Reagan*, 74.

"nice and good . . .": Reagan, Nancy, *My Turn*, 78.

"I had been . . .": Reagan, Nancy, *My Turn*, 80.

"If Nancy Davis . . .": Reagan, Nancy, *My Turn*, 103.

"When I say . . .": Colacello, *Ronnie and Nancy*.

"What is Ronald . . .": Reagan, Nancy, *My Turn*, 87.

"Ronnie is an . . .": Reagan, Nancy, *My Turn*, 89.

"But it can . . .": Reagan, Nancy, *My Turn*, 91.

"Both my brother . . .": Bosch, "The American Experience."

"I'd emphasize that . . ." and "Those GE tours . . .": Reagan, *An
    American Life*, 129.

CHAPTER SIX

"Mermie, I really . . .": Reagan, Maureen, *First Father, First Daughter*,
    138–39.

"It's time we . . .": Reagan, "A Time for Choosing."

"I can't remember . . .": Reagan, *An American Life*, 145.

"For about two . . .": Reagan, Nancy, *My Turn*, 110.

"Sure, the man . . .": Cannon, *Governor Reagan*, 149.

"Once I got . . .": Reagan, *An American Life*, 152.

CHAPTER SEVEN

"As funny as . . .": Reagan, *An American Life*, 155.

"We were amateurs": Cannon, *Governor Reagan*, 184.

"How could you . . .": Reagan, Nancy, *My Turn*, 139.

"We are going . . .": Cannon, *Governor Reagan*, 174–75.

"I realized after . . .": Reagan, *An American Life*, 170.

"When I began . . .": Reagan, *An American Life*, 171.

"When I got . . ." and "In Hollywood, Nancy . . .": Reagan, *An American Life*, 166–67.

"I also discovered . . .": Reagan, *An American Life*, 171.

"I'd been governor . . .": Reagan, *An American Life*, 176.

"Clearly [he was] ambitious . . .": Cannon, *Governor Reagan*, 258.

"When the delegation . . .": Reagan, *An American Life*, 179.

"We have some . . ." and "Shhhhhhhhhhh!": Cannon, *Governor Reagan*, 285.

"By the end . . .": Reagan, *An American Life*, 184.

"I have never . . .": Reagan, *An American Life*, 185.

CHAPTER EIGHT

"His form of . . ." and "He would go . . .": Bosch, "The American Experience."

"the only adult . . .": Cannon, *Governor Reagan*, 80.

"He just finds . . .": Cannon, *President Reagan*, 194.

"I never knew . . ." and "I knew him . . .": Cannon, *Governor Reagan*, 79.

"For Ronnie, this . . .": Reagan, Nancy, *My Turn*, 151.

"I didn't automatically . . .": Reagan, *An American Life*, 196.

"This was frustrating . . ." and "I've been speaking . . .": Reagan, Nancy, *My Turn*, 152.

"The question was . . .": Bosch, "The American Experience."

"The cause goes . . .": Reagan, Nancy, *My Turn*, 169.

"I wasn't the . . .": Reagan, *An American Life*, 203–4.

"There you go . . .": Cannon, *Governor Reagan*, 505.

"Are you better . . .": Patterson, *Restless Giant*, 148.

"big leagues . . .": Cannon, *President Reagan*, 91.

"I'm the one . . .": Cannon, *President Reagan*, 99.

"sense of unreality" and "Both of us . . .": Cannon, *President Reagan*, 73.

CHAPTER NINE

"A most wonderful . . .": Reagan, *An American Life*, 226.

"We must act . . ." and "Let us renew . . .": McPherson, *To the Best of My Ability*, 443–44.

"I think it . . .": Reagan, *An American Life*, 228–29.

"I keep thinking . . .": Reagan, *The Reagan Diaries*, 8.

"He assembled people . . .": Bosch, "The American Experience."

"Whenever somebody told . . .": Cannon, *President Reagan*, 148.

"whenever work was . . .": Reagan, *An American Life*, 249.

"After all our . . .": Reagan, *An American Life*, 250.

"I'm not going . . .": Reeves, *President Reagan*, 29.

"There's been a . . ." and "George, I'm going . . .": Reagan, Nancy, *My Turn*, 1.

"He's been hit . . ." and "Mike. They don't . . .": Reagan, Nancy, *My Turn*, 2.

"Ronnie looked pale . . .": Reagan, Nancy, *My Turn*, 3–4.

"Who's minding the . . .": Broder, "Reagan Wounded by Assailant's Bullet."

"I cannot answer . . ." and "Constitutionally, gentlemen, you . . .": Reeves, *President Reagan*, 40.

"Getting shot hurts . . .": Reagan, *The Reagan Diaries*, 12.

"A new legend . . .": Broder, "End of a Dream."

"That reception was . . .": Reeves, *President Reagan*, 56.

"If it makes . . .": Reagan, Nancy, *My Turn*, 43.

"Iron underwear": Reagan, *An American Life*, 262.

"What he preaches . . .": Reeves, *President Reagan*, 71.

"That left seventeen . . .": Greider, *The Education of David Stockman.*

"The Justice Department . . ." and "Bill is right . . .": Reeves, *President Reagan*, 29.

"The federal government . . .": Stockman, *The Triumph of Politics*, 275.

"That I was . . .": Reagan, Nancy, *My Turn*, 21.

"I wish the . . .": Reagan, Nancy, *My Turn*, 31.

"I know what . . .": Reeves, *President Reagan*, 132.

CHAPTER TEN

"The West won't . . .": Gaddis, *The Cold War*, 223.

"It is the . . .": Cannon, *President Reagan*, 271.

"My motives were . . .": Bosch, "The American Experience."

"I'm afraid our . . .": Reagan, *The Reagan Diaries*, 117.

"El Salvador and . . .": Reagan, *An American Life*, 238–39.

"are . . . the moral": Reeves, *President Reagan*, 245.

"It was far . . .": Cannon, *President Reagan*, 127.

"The Holocaust, I . . .": Reagan, *An American Life*, 410.

"Israel's response was . . .": Reagan, *An American Life*, 419.

"Boy, that guy . . .": Cannon, *President Reagan*, 344.

"Menachem, this is . . ." "Mr. President, I . . ." and "I didn't know . . .":
    Cannon, *President Reagan*, 350.

"As the summer . . .": Reagan, *An American Life*, 435.

"purpose is not . . .": Cannon, *President Reagan*, 357.

"We were both . . .": Reagan, *The Reagan Diaries*, 147.

"Are we in . . ." and "America is a . . .": Reagan, *An American Life*, 447.

"I yearned for . . .": Reagan, Nancy, *My Turn*, 224.

"Ronnie has always . . .": Reagan, Nancy, *My Turn*, 226.

"I will not . . .": Cannon, *President Reagan*, 486.

CHAPTER ELEVEN

"A President in . . .": Reeves, *President Reagan*, 237.

"I approved the . . .": Reagan, *An American Life*, 488.

"Don Regan was . . .": Bosch, "The American Experience."

"They told me . . .": Reagan, Nancy, *My Turn*, 269.

"The press has . . .": Reagan, *The Reagan Diaries*, 316.

"Americans were still . . .": Reagan, *An American Life*, 498.

"I learned how . . .": Reagan, *An American Life*, 490–91.

"Does this mean . . .": Reagan, Nancy, *My Turn*, 232.

"Some strange soundings . . .": Reagan, *The Reagan Diaries*, 343.

"He wanted to . . .": Cannon, *President Reagan*, 541.

"I received a . . .": Reagan, *The Reagan Diaries*, 350.

"Lord I hope . . .": Reagan, *The Reagan Diaries*, 369.

"As we shook . . .": Reagan, *An American Life*, 635.

"I read it . . ." "You've trashed us . . ." and "I think Patti's . . .":
Reagan, Nancy, *My Turn*, 141.

"He's brought a . . .": Cannon, *President Reagan*, 687.

"I realized he . . ." and "The meeting is . . .": Reagan, *An American
Life*, 679.

"Can't we do . . ." and "It's too late . . .": Cannon, *President Reagan*, 690.

"This whole irresponsible . . .": Reagan, *The Reagan Diaries*, 450.

"We did not . . .": Cannon, *President Reagan*, 608.

"North didn't tell . . .": Reagan, *The Reagan Diaries*, 453.

"This whole thing . . .": Cannon, *President Reagan*, 625.

"I felt I . . .": Reagan, *An American Life*, 532.

"He never had . . .": Cannon, *President Reagan*, 639.

"A few months . . .": Cannon, *President Reagan*, 655.

"I still believe . . .": Reagan, *An American Life*, 540 -41.

"Reagan is a . . .": Bosch, "The American Experience."

"I think the . . .": Reagan, Nancy, *My Turn*, 244.

"My breast is gone . . ." and "It doesn't matter . . .": Reagan, *An
American Life*, 695.

"General Secretary Gorbachev . . .": Cannon, *President Reagan*, 695.

"Freedom is the . . .": Cannon, *President Reagan*, 706.

CHAPTER TWELVE

"There's our little . . .": Cannon, *President Reagan*, 5.

"Then home & . . .": Reagan, *The Reagan Diaries*, 693.

"At the moment . . .": Cannon, *President Reagan*, xv.

BIBLIOGRAPHY

Barrett, Lawrence. *Gambling with History: Ronald Reagan in the White House*. New York: Doubleday, 1983.

Black, Earl, and Merle Black. *The Rise of Southern Republicans*. Cambridge, Mass.: The Belknap Press of Harvard University Press, 2002.

Bosch, Adriana, and Austin Hoyt, Producers. "The American Experience: Reagan." A production of WGBH Boston for The American Experience/PBS, 1998.

Broder, David S. "End of a Dream." *Washington Post*, April 1, 1981.

―――. "Reagan Wounded by Assailant's Bullet: Three Others Shot; President's Prognosis Excellent." *Washington Post*, March 31, 1981.

Cannon, Lou. *Governor Reagan: His Rise to Power*. New York: Public Affairs, 2003.

―――. *President Reagan: The Role of a Lifetime*. New York: Public Affairs, 2000.

Colacello, Bob. "Ronnie and Nancy." *Vanity Fair*, July–August, 1998.

Cramer, Richard Ben. *What It Takes: The Way to the White House*. New York: Random House, 1992.

Evans, Thomas W. *The Education of Ronald Reagan: The General Electric Years and the Untold Story of His Conversion to Conservatism*. New York: Columbia University Press, 2006.

Farrell, John A. *Tip O'Neill and the Democratic Century*. New York: Little, Brown, 2001.

Frank, Mitch. *Understanding September 11th: Answering Questions about the Attacks on America*. New York: Viking Children's Books, 2002.

Gaddis, John Lewis. *The Cold War: A New History*. New York: The Penguin Press, 2005.

Gorbachev, Mikhail. *Memoirs*. New York: Doubleday, 1995.

Gravitz, Herbert L., and Julie D. Bowden. *Recovery: A Guide for Adult Children of Alcoholics*. New York: Simon & Schuster, 1985.

Greider, William. "The Education of David Stockman." *The Atlantic*, December 1981.

Inouye, Daniel K., and Lee H. Hamilton. *Report of the Congressional Committees Investigating the Iran-Contra Affair*. Washington, D.C.: Government Printing Office, 1987.

McPherson, James M., ed. *To the Best of My Ability: The*

American Presidents. New York: Dorling Kindersley, 2000.

Oberdorfer, Don. "At Reykjavik, Soviets were prepared and U.S. improvised." *Washington Post*, February 16, 1987.

Patterson, James T. *Restless Giant: The United States from Watergate to Bush v. Gore*. New York: Oxford University Press, 2005.

"Prime Minister issues harsh criticism of U.S." The Associated Press, December 20, 1981.

Reagan, Maureen. *First Father, First Daughter: A Memoir*. Boston: Little, Brown, 1989.

Reagan, Nancy, with William Novak. *My Turn: The Memoirs of Nancy Reagan*. New York: Random House, 1989.

Reagan, Ronald. "A Time for Choosing," address on behalf of Senator Barry Goldwater. Ronald Reagan Presidential Foundation & Library, October 27, 1964.

———. Address at Commencement Exercises at Eureka College in Illinois, May 9, 1982.

———, with Robert Lindsey. *An American Life*. New York: Pocket Books, 1990.

———. *The Reagan Diaries*. Edited by Douglas Brinkley. New York: HarperCollins, 2007.

Reeves, Richard. *President Reagan: The Triumph of Imagination*. New York: Simon & Schuster Paperbacks, 2006.

Regan, Donald T. *For the Record: From Wall Street to Washington.* New York: Harcourt Brace Jovanovich, 1988.

Skinner, Kiron K., Martin Anderson, and Annelise Anderson, eds. *Reagan: A Life in Letters.* New York: Simon & Schuster, 2004.

Stockman, David Allan. *The Triumph of Politics: How the Reagan Revolution Failed.* New York: Harper & Row, 1986.

Wills, Gary. *Reagan's America: Innocents at Home.* New York: Doubleday & Company, 1987.

INDEX

Note: Page numbers in *italics* refer to photographs.

Photo Credits

ACKNOWLEDGMENTS

I SPENT MANY hours at my computer in the past year griping that it would have been easier to write about a man who didn't live so long. The truth is, Ronald Reagan was a more complex man than most people give him credit for. Digging deep to try to find his inner nature was a wonderful challenge.

Keeping me sane were all the brilliant and patient people at Viking. I want to thank them all, particularly my editor, Catherine Frank, whose intelligence, insight, and level-headed approach are invaluable. And special thanks to Jim Hoover, Nico Medina, Janet Pascal, Kate Renner, and Regina Hayes.

And thanks to my parents for allowing me to keep that *Time* subscription, and to fill my room with Reagan memorabilia; and to my junior high history teachers who put up with my oddness and nicknamed me Alex P. Keaton.